Withdrawn

Withdrawn

SKIN CONDITIONS
FROM ACNE TO ECZEMA

By Donna Reynolds

Portions of this book originally appeared in *Acne* by Bonnie Juettner.

LUCENT PRESS

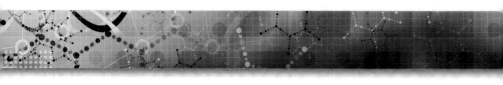

Published in 2019 by
Lucent Press, an Imprint of Greenhaven Publishing, LLC
353 3rd Avenue
Suite 255
New York, NY 10010

Designer: Deanna Paternostro
Editor: Jennifer Lombardo

Library of Congress Cataloging-in-Publication Data

Names: Reynolds, Donna, author.
Title: Skin conditions : from acne to eczema / Donna Reynolds.
Description: New York : Lucent, [2019] | Series: Diseases and disorders |
  Includes bibliographical references and index.
Identifiers: LCCN 2018028521 (print) | LCCN 2018031486 (ebook) | ISBN
  9781534564817 (eBook) | ISBN 9781534564800 (library bound book) | ISBN
  9781534564794 (pbk. book)
Subjects: LCSH: Skin–Diseases. | Skin–Diseases–Treatment.
Classification: LCC RL71 (ebook) | LCC RL71 .R49 2019 (print) | DDC
  616.5–dc23
LC record available at https://lccn.loc.gov/2018028521
Printed in the United States of America

CPSIA compliance information: Batch #BW19KL: For further information contact Greenhaven Publishing LLC, New York,
New York, at 1-844-317-7404.

Please visit our website, www.greenhavenpublishing.com. For a free color catalog of all our
high-quality books, call toll free 1-844-317-7404 or fax 1-844-317-7405.

CONTENTS

Illness is an unfortunate part of life, and it is one that is often misunderstood. Thanks to advances in science and technology, people have been aware for many years that diseases such as the flu, pneumonia, and chicken pox are caused by viruses and bacteria. These diseases all cause physical symptoms that people can see and understand, and many people have dealt with these diseases themselves. However, sometimes diseases that were previously unknown in most of the world turn into epidemics and spread across the globe. Without an awareness of the method by which these diseases are spread—through the air, through human waste or fluids, through sexual contact, or by some other method—people cannot take the proper precautions to prevent further contamination. Panic often accompanies epidemics as a result of this lack of knowledge.

Knowledge is power in the case of mental disorders, as well. Mental disorders are just as common as physical disorders, but due to a lack of awareness among the general public, they are often stigmatized. Scientists have studied them for years and have found that they are generally caused by hormonal imbalances in the brain, but they have not yet determined with certainty what causes those imbalances or how to fix them. Because even mild mental illness is stigmatized in Western society, many people prefer not to talk about it.

Chronic pain disorders are also not well understood—even by researchers—and do not yet have foolproof treatments. People who have a mental disorder or a disease or disorder that causes them to feel chronic pain can be the target of uninformed

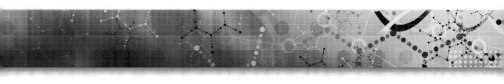

opinions. People who do not have these disorders sometimes struggle to understand how difficult it can be to deal with the symptoms. These disorders are often termed "invisible illnesses" because no one can see the symptoms; this leads many people to doubt that they exist or are serious problems. Additionally, people who have an undiagnosed disorder may understand that they are experiencing the world in a different way than their peers, but they have no one to turn to for answers.

Misinformation about all kinds of ailments is often spread through personal anecdotes, social media, and even news sources. This series aims to present accurate information about both physical and mental conditions so young adults will have a better understanding of them. Each volume discusses the symptoms of a particular disease or disorder, ways it is currently being treated, and the research that is being done to understand it further. Advice for people who may be suffering from the disorder is included, as well as information for their loved ones about how best to support them.

With fully cited quotes, a list of recommended books and websites for further research, and informational charts, this series provides young adults with a factual introduction to common illnesses. By learning more about these ailments, they will be better able to prevent the spread of contagious diseases, show compassion to people who are dealing with invisible illnesses, and take charge of their own health.

UNDERSTANDING SKIN CONDITIONS

Although most people do not think of skin as an organ, it is the largest organ in the human body. Its job is to protect and contain the parts of the body that keep people alive. It also plays a role in maintaining the correct body temperature and gives people the sense of touch.

Like any other organ, the skin can fall victim to diseases and disorders. Since it is the first line of defense for the body, it is constantly exposed to things that can cause or worsen these conditions: wind, rain, germs, chemicals, and many more. However, some conditions are caused by factors inside the body.

Skin is not just about looks. It plays an important role in keeping people healthy.

Skin Conditions with Internal Causes

Some of the most common skin conditions are partially or totally caused by factors inside the body. None of them are life-threatening, although they often cause discomfort and embarrassment.

Acne is the most common skin condition in the world, and it is often caused by a combination of factors, such as changes in hormones or brain chemicals, as well as too much oil production and bacteria on the skin. Acne can affect people of all ages, but it is most common in young adults. Dermatologists (doctors who specialize in treating skin problems) estimate that about 80 percent of people between the ages of 11 and 30 have acne at some point in their lives.

Another common problem is eczema, which is actually a group of skin conditions. There are at least 11 different conditions that can cause eczema, which is characterized by red, itchy rashes in places such as the face, feet, and backs of the knees. About 15 percent of children and 2 to 4 percent of adults have eczema, although in adults it is generally more severe. Its exact causes are unknown, but researchers believe it happens because of a combination of genetic and environmental factors. Genes are bits of deoxyribonucleic acid (DNA), which contains all the information that makes a person who they are. Genes control things such as eye color, whether a person is right- or left-handed, and whether they are at risk of developing certain diseases. In the past, scientists believed one gene controlled each factor, but now they know that in most cases, something as simple as eye color is caused by hundreds of genes working together. Someone who has the gene or genes for eczema inherited them from their parents. Not everyone who has the genes will develop the disorder; something in the environment must activate it. Researchers are still trying to identify the environmental and genetic factors involved.

A third common disorder is psoriasis. This is a problem with the body's immune system, which is the system that fights off disease. In an autoimmune disease such as psoriasis, the immune system attacks itself, mistakenly believing the body's own cells are foreign invaders such as bacteria. About 3 percent of people in the world and about 2 percent of Americans have psoriasis, which is characterized by patches of itchy, scaly skin.

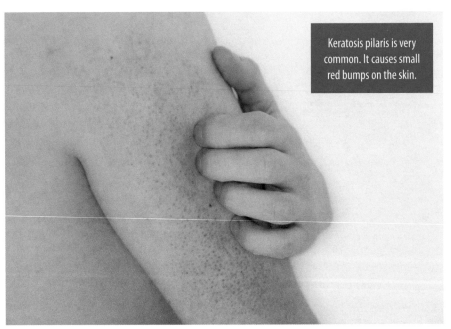

Keratosis pilaris is very common. It causes small red bumps on the skin.

Other common skin conditions with internal causes include keratosis pilaris, vitiligo, and moles. Keratosis pilaris is extremely common, but many people who have it do not know it has a name. It is a genetic disorder that causes tiny, red, sometimes itchy bumps on the skin, especially on the upper arms and front of the thighs. More than 50 percent of young adults are estimated to have this condition. It is caused by a buildup of dead skin cells in the pores. Vitiligo is a disease that causes skin cells to lose their color, or pigment. Although it can happen to anyone, it is most noticeable in people with dark skin, such as African American or Indian people. Its cause is unknown, but some researchers believe it is an autoimmune disease because it often occurs in people with other autoimmune diseases. About 1 percent of people worldwide have this condition. Moles are skin cells that grow in a cluster instead of evenly spread out on the skin, which makes them darker than the surrounding skin. They are often raised as well. Although some are cancerous, many are harmless. Depending on where on the body they are—for instance, on the face—someone may choose to have them removed even if they are not deadly. According to the American Academy of Dermatology (AAD), almost every adult has at least one mole.

Skin Conditions with External Causes

There are dozens of other skin conditions—many of them very common—that are caused by external factors such as bacteria, viruses, and allergic reactions. One of the most common is warts. These are caused by the human papillomavirus (HPV). HPV is most commonly known as a sexually transmitted disease (STD), but there are more than 100 different strains of the virus, and less than half of them affect the genitals. A wart on the hand or sole of the foot generally cannot be transferred to the genitals. Cold sores, which appear around the lips, are also caused by a virus better known as an STD: herpes simplex, more commonly known simply as herpes. However, unlike the various HPV strains, herpes can affect multiple parts of the body. If a person with an open cold sore performs oral sex on their partner, they risk giving their partner genital herpes.

Cold sores and warts are harmless and often go away on their own, although treatment may make them disappear faster. However, a bacterial infection called cellulitis is considered a medical emergency. According to Healthline, the infection, which is frequently painful, "may first appear as a red, swollen area that feels hot and tender to the touch. The redness and swelling often spread rapidly ... In most cases, the skin on the lower legs is affected, although the infection can occur anywhere on your body or face."[1] The infection starts on the surface of the skin, but if left untreated, it can end up spreading to the lymph nodes and bloodstream, and it could quickly become deadly.

Fungi can also cause skin conditions. Ringworm is a skin infection caused by a mold-like fungus that lives on hair, nails, and dead skin. It creates a round patch, or ring, which is how it got its name. It can also cause hair to fall out. On the feet, it is known as athlete's foot; in the groin, it is often called jock itch. Ringworm is extremely contagious and can be spread by touching an infected person or animal—or even items they touched, such as towels or hairbrushes—or by standing barefoot in soil that contains the fungus.

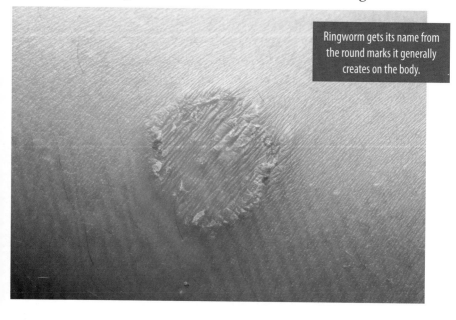

Ringworm gets its name from the round marks it generally creates on the body.

While these viruses and bacteria are directly responsible for causing skin conditions, other bacteria and viruses cause diseases with multiple symptoms that include a rash or other skin problem. These include chicken pox, shingles, and lupus, among others. Allergic reactions, too, can cause a rash. An allergy is an oversensitivity to a certain material, which the body treats as a foreign invader. For instance, people who are allergic to certain foods may break out in hives if they eat that food. Hives are swollen bumps that appear on the skin, most often because of an allergy. They generally disappear on their own, but if they are very severe, they may require emergency treatment, as they can interfere with a person's breathing if they affect the throat or tongue.

There are many other skin conditions, some less common than others. However, many of them are not deadly or contagious, and nearly all can be treated with medical help. Some even go away on their own.

Skin Conditions and Self-Esteem

Although most skin conditions will not kill someone, they can cause pain and itching, among other symptoms. However, one of the most severe issues people with skin conditions face is embarrassment. When a skin condition such as psoriasis or acne develops on a highly visible part of the body, such as the face or hands, it can lower people's self-esteem. The more severe the symptoms are, the more likely they are to feel this way. Like other physical traits—weight and height, for example—the state of a person's skin can affect how that person feels about themselves. Teenagers, especially, may view a skin condition as more noticeable than it really is—a pimple that others do not see may appear enormous to the eyes of an adolescent examining their appearance in the mirror. Psychological researchers estimate that up to one-third of a person's self-esteem relies on their appearance, especially in a society that seems to value beauty.

Although acne itself is generally not a serious medical problem, psychologists say that about 50 percent of teenagers with acne develop psychological conditions stemming from it. Sandra Osborne remembered how her 15-year-old son, Sterling, reacted to his breakouts. "He is good-looking, but when the acne got bad he would say 'Why would anyone want to go out with me?'" she recalled. "His confidence was low."[2] Teens with acne often have increased levels of social anxiety, low self-esteem, and depression.

The same issues can affect people with other skin conditions as well. According to the AAD, "Major depression is one of the main results of chronic skin disorders."[3] People who are affected are also more

People often feel self-conscious about their skin.

likely to have suicidal thoughts and anger problems.

Adults with skin conditions frequently also have a hard time feeling confident in social situations. Journalist Jess Weiner said, "The blemish becomes magnified, at least in your own mind."[4] Weiner covered her acne with makeup for years. Then one day, she decided to go without her trademark concealer—and no one seemed to notice the difference. The acne, she realized, was far more visible to her than it was to anyone else.

Some people, such as those with mild acne or vitiligo, are able to cover their skin condition with makeup. Others, such as those with psoriasis or eczema, do not have this option, especially if the condition gets worse when they touch it. However, some people choose not to use makeup even if they have the option, deciding instead to embrace the things that make them unique. In the 21st century, attitudes about beauty are slowly changing. Today, more people realize that people's differences are what make them beautiful and that someone who does not look like a supermodel can still be beautiful.

CHAPTER ONE

SYMPTOMS OF COMMON CONDITIONS

The symptoms of skin conditions vary widely. Some, such as acne, are easy to spot and generally do not require a doctor's diagnosis. Others can have symptoms that are shared among several different disorders, making it difficult for an individual to figure out the exact cause. For instance, dandruff—itchiness and flakes of dead skin on the scalp—can be caused by not shampooing enough; an allergy to certain products; a yeast called malassezia, which irritates the scalp and causes too much skin to grow; or a condition called seborrheic dermatitis, which causes a form of eczema on the scalp. It can be difficult for someone to figure out exactly what the cause is, so a visit to a dermatologist may be necessary.

The Parts of the Skin

In order to understand skin conditions, it is important to understand the skin itself. It consists of three layers: the epidermis, dermis, and hypodermis (also called subcutaneous tissue). The epidermis is the outer layer, the surface where conditions become visible. The dermis is a thicker layer, housing a network of nerve endings, blood vessels, hair follicles, and sweat and sebaceous, or oil, glands. Under the dermis lies the hypodermis, which includes a layer of fat that insulates the body and cushions it from bumps and falls. Altogether, the skin makes up about 15 percent of a person's body mass. It is the main organ in the integumentary system, which also includes the hair, nails, and sebaceous and sweat glands of the dermis. (Not everything in the dermis is part of the integumentary system. For example, nerve endings are part of the nervous system, and blood vessels are part of the circulatory system.)

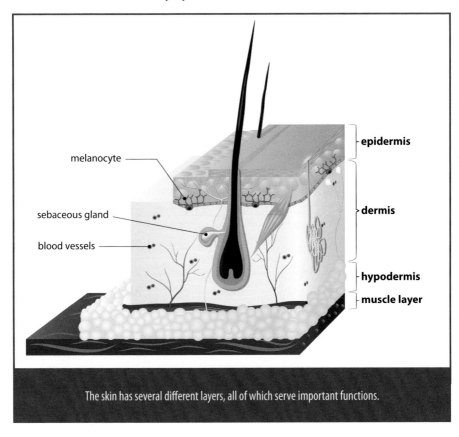

melanocyte

sebaceous gland

blood vessels

epidermis

dermis

hypodermis

muscle layer

The skin has several different layers, all of which serve important functions.

The skin covers and protects the body's internal organs, but it also does much more than that. It helps the body maintain homeostasis. This means that the skin helps the body stay in balance by helping it maintain a healthy temperature and by excreting substances that the body needs to get rid of. The skin removes water, salt, and waste substances—such as a protein called urea—from the bloodstream, and the sweat glands excrete them in sweat. (Most urea is excreted in urine, but a small amount is excreted in sweat.) At the same time, the body's sebaceous glands secrete an oil called sebum, which keeps the skin from drying out and protects it from germs. When people refer to "oily skin," this means their skin produces too much sebum.

The skin's sebaceous glands and sweat glands are located in the skin's deep inner layer, called the dermis. Each person has between 2 million and 5 million glands—more than 10 glands for every square millimeter of skin. The sebaceous glands are located within hair follicles, which are small sacs in the skin out of which hairs grow. Each hair follicle is lined with cells from the epidermis, the skin's outer layer. The sebaceous glands open out into the follicles, providing sebum to moisturize the hair as it grows. There are hair follicles all over the body; tiny, fine hairs, called vellus hairs, grow all over the body, even on the face, chest, and back. It is sometimes called "peach fuzz," and it is often unnoticeable unless someone looks very closely. In places such as the arms, legs, and pubic area, vellus hair turns into terminal hair, which is the same type of hair that grows on a person's head.

How Acne Forms

Acne begins in the sebaceous glands. Because there is such an extensive network of sebaceous glands throughout the skin, it is possible for a person with acne to develop a fairly extensive and severe case of the condition. Acne generally begins when the sebaceous glands suddenly start to increase the amount of sebum they produce. Sebum production increases during puberty and during other hormonal events such as menstruation. The extra sebum sometimes causes dead epidermal skin cells to stick together, forming a plug that dermatologists call a comedo. The resulting blemish is then called a comedone.

Doctors do not know why acne forms in particular hair follicles and not others. "To me, one of the most incredible mysteries is how come only some follicles are involved at any given time," remarked Pennsylvania dermatologist Albert Kligman. "You've got thousands of sebaceous follicles on your face … But maybe you've only got ten or fifteen or twenty comedones. Here's one follicle with a comedo, and right next door, here's one that's normal. Why is that? Whatever it is, we simply don't know."[5]

Superficial cases of acne are mild and stay close to the surface of the skin. The comedo blocks the opening of one of the skin's pores. If the pore is closed, the blocked pore is called a whitehead. If the pore is open, the melanin, or pigment, in the comedo reacts chemically with oxygen in the air. It causes the comedo to darken, so this kind of blocked pore is called a blackhead. In blackheads and whiteheads, there is no redness, or inflammation, so blackheads and whiteheads are considered noninflammatory acne. Many people think they have a lot of blackheads all over their nose and cheeks, but those small black dots that can be seen when someone leans in very close to the mirror are called sebaceous filaments. They are the tips of sebaceous glands. Sebaceous filaments—which are a normal, healthy part of the face that everyone has—can be distinguished from blackheads because they are smooth to the touch, while blackheads are raised.

For people with mild cases of acne, the acne may consist only of blackheads and whiteheads. In moderate or severe cases, though, acne continues to progress, and the blackheads or whiteheads become infected and inflamed. The infection is caused by

Propionibacterium acnes (*P. acnes*), a bacterium that normally lives deep in the skin. An infected blemish will turn red and begin to swell in size. At this point, it is called a pimple.

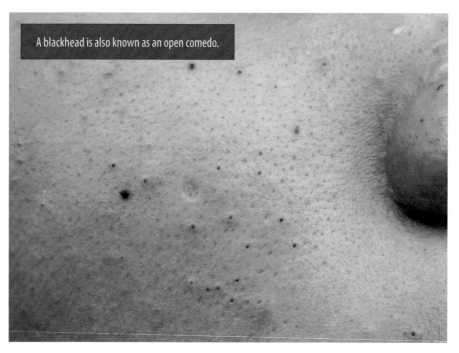

A blackhead is also known as an open comedo.

Once a pimple has become infected, it is no longer considered a whitehead or a blackhead. Instead, it gets a different name, depending on its appearance and location. A small, firm, red bump is called a papule. It does not contain any obvious pus and is located relatively near the surface of the skin. A papule that is full of obvious pus is called a pustule. The pus in a pustule tends to be white and gooey. It is made up of dead white blood cells. Pimples that are located deep under the surface of the skin are called nodules. They are hard to the touch; they can be tender and painful, and they take a long time to heal. Cysts, like nodules, are deep under the skin, but unlike nodules, they are filled with pus. This makes them soft to the touch, although pressing on them may be painful. According to Acne.com, "Acne cysts develop when the contents of your comedones … 'spill' into surrounding areas of your skin. In an effort to fix the situation, which your body perceives as an attack, the local immune system responds by producing pus."[6]

Dermatologists classify acne according to whether it consists mostly of whiteheads and blackheads or whether it tends to produce cysts. People who get only a few blemishes at a time and who tend to get mostly whiteheads and blackheads are said to have mild acne. People who sometimes get cysts and who tend to have more frequent lesions have moderate acne. People who get mostly cystic acne and who get many lesions at any given time have severe acne.

Many people try to get rid of whiteheads, blackheads, pustules, and cysts by squeezing them. However, doing this can push bacteria deeper into the skin and leaves scars. Dermatologists have special tools to remove blackheads and cysts if necessary.

Diseases That Cause Skin Problems

There are dozens of diseases that come with a rash or other type of skin condition. For instance, chicken pox, a common childhood illness caused by a virus, is characterized by the itchy red spots that appear on the body, along with fever, headache, and tiredness. Lupus, an autoimmune disease, causes a distinctive "facial rash that resembles the wings of a butterfly unfolding across both cheeks."[1] Its other symptoms include tiredness, fever, joint pain, chest pain, and memory loss. Lyme disease, which is caused by a bacterium that is transmitted through tick bites, also creates a distinctive rash—one that is shaped like a bulls-eye. These are only a few of the many diseases that include a skin condition as a symptom. Generally, once the disease is cured, the skin clears up. However, in some instances—such as when someone scratches their chicken pox blisters—scarring can occur.

1. Mayo Clinic Staff, "Lupus," Mayo Clinic, October 25, 2017. www.mayoclinic.org/diseases-conditions/lupus/symptoms-causes/syc-20365789.

Symptoms of Eczema

According to MedicineNet,

> *Rather than a specific health condition, eczema is a reaction pattern that the skin produces in a number of diseases. It begins as red, raised tiny blisters containing a clear fluid atop red, elevated plaques. When the blisters break, the affected skin will weep and ooze. In older eczema … the blisters are less prominent and the skin is thickened, elevated, and scaling. Eczema almost always is very itchy.*[7]

Medically, most forms of eczema are called dermatitis. Some forms of dermatitis include atopic, which is the most common form of eczema; irritant, which is when the skin is washed too often or comes into contact with a toxic substance; allergic contact, which is a reaction to an allergen (for instance, the rash that develops when someone touches poison ivy); stasis, which affects the swollen lower legs of people with poor blood circulation in the legs; and seborrheic, which causes a rash on the scalp and face.

Atopic dermatitis (shown here) is the most common form of eczema.

Other conditions that can cause eczema include:

- pompholyx, or dyshidrotic eczema, which generally affects only the hands and feet
- lichen simplex chronicus, or neurodermatitis, which creates thick, itchy patches of skin that are caused by people scratching their eczema
- nummular dermatitis, or discoid eczema, which, unlike other forms of the disorder, creates raised, coin-shaped spots that may or may not itch
- xerotic dermatitis, or asteatotic dermatitis, which makes the affected skin cracked, crusty, and swollen

Some people believe eczema is contagious, but dermatitis cannot be transferred between humans. However, some fungal infections can cause an eczema-like rash, as can scabies, which is an infestation of small bugs called itch mites. Both of these examples are contagious. A dermatologist can determine whether someone's condition is contagious or not.

Eczema can be confusing because not everyone has the same symptoms, and the same person may have eczema in multiple areas on their body.

How Psoriasis Forms

Psoriasis is an autoimmune disorder, and like acne, it starts underneath the top layer of skin. In someone without the disorder, it takes about a month to produce new skin cells and get rid of the old ones. However, with psoriasis, "your immune system is overactive, triggering skin inflammation and causing skin cells to be produced much faster than normal. New skin cells are pushed to the skin's surface in 3 to 4 days instead of the usual 28 to 30."[8] Because the body cannot shed the old skin cells fast enough, this dead skin piles up on top of itself, causing a raised, scaly, itchy bump called a plaque. It is generally red and covered in silvery, scale-like skin.

Warts and Cold Sores

Warts and cold sores are two very common skin conditions that can be caused by viruses. Unlike a disease such as chicken pox, these viruses generally do not cause other symptoms.

Warts are a highly contagious skin condition caused by certain strains of the human papillomavirus (HPV). The virus can be transmitted when someone with broken skin, such as a cut or small scratch, comes into contact with the virus. This can happen if they shake the hand of someone with a wart or touch something the other person has touched—for example, by walking barefoot, especially in moist places such as swimming pools. Plantar warts appear on the soles of the feet, while common warts appear in other places, such as the hands or face. Most warts can be identified by their cauliflower-like appearance. They will often go away on their own, but they can be treated more quickly with over-the-counter (OTC) medications such as patches. A dermatologist can use liquid butane to freeze especially stubborn warts. Most people have had a wart at some point in their life.

Cold sores are another highly contagious skin condition. They are caused by the herpes simplex virus (HSV-1). Like warts, they are transmitted through direct contact with the skin or by touching something the cold sore has touched—for instance, when people share drinks. Some people get them as children when a family friend or relative who has an open cold sore kisses them. They are most contagious when the blister appears and right after it bursts. HSV-1 cannot be spread through skin-to-skin contact after the cold sore has healed, but it can be transmitted through the saliva at any time. Once the virus is inside the body, it never goes away, although cold sores come and go and can be treated with medication. Some people experience outbreaks more often than others, and some people who have the virus never get a cold sore. Researchers are unsure exactly why, but they believe stress is one factor that plays a role.

Plaque psoriasis is the most common form of psoriasis; experts estimate that 80 percent of people with psoriasis have this type. However, there are several others. They are:

- nail psoriasis, which makes fingernails and toenails cracked and discolored

- guttate psoriasis, the second-most common type, which typically appears in childhood or young adulthood and is characterized by small, red, dot-like lesions
- inverse psoriasis, which gets its name because it appears to be the opposite of plaque psoriasis. Rather than raised lesions, it shows up as smooth, red, shiny patches in the folds of the body—for instance, behind the knees or in the armpits.
- pustular psoriasis, which causes pimple-like pustules to appear on the skin, most commonly on the hands and feet
- erythrodermic psoriasis, "a particularly severe form … that leads to widespread, fiery redness over most of the body. It can cause severe itching and pain, and make the skin come off in sheets."[9] It is a rare condition, but it is considered a medical emergency because it can be life-threatening.

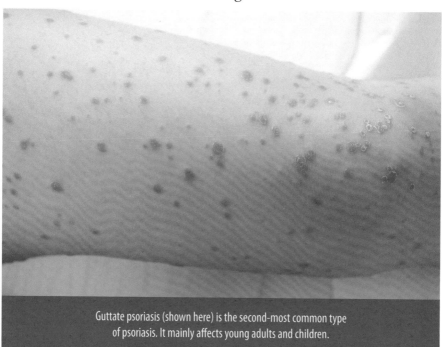

Guttate psoriasis (shown here) is the second-most common type of psoriasis. It mainly affects young adults and children.

Like eczema, psoriasis is not contagious and in most cases, is not life-threatening. A dermatologist can generally diagnose psoriasis just by looking at it, but in some cases where it appears similar to eczema or another disorder, a biopsy may be performed. This is when the doctor takes a small sample of skin and looks at it under a microscope. Skin that has psoriasis will look thicker and more inflamed under the microscope than skin with eczema.

CHAPTER TWO

CAUSES OF COMMON CONDITIONS

For some of the most common skin conditions, including acne, eczema, and psoriasis, doctors are unsure of the exact causes. They know certain things, such as genetics or environmental factors, play a role, but it is often difficult or impossible for them to say who is likely to develop one of these conditions. Research into these areas is ongoing.

Acne and Hormones

While a person can develop acne at any age, it is most common during puberty. It is thought that nearly all teenagers experience acne—whether it is mild, moderate, or severe—at some point. During puberty, two glands in the brain, the hypothalamus and the pituitary gland, release hormones that have a dramatic effect on the body, including the skin. Glands are a type of organ, just as the heart, lung, kidneys, and even the skin itself are organs. The hypothalamus and pituitary glands are located in the brain, but other glands are located throughout the body.

Certain glands, rather than having their own function, exist for the purpose of regulating the work of other organs. They do this by releasing hormones—chemicals that tell different organs in the body what to do. Glands operate throughout a person's life, not just during puberty. For example, the thymus, a gland in the chest, responds to infections. It releases hormones that stimulate white blood cells to mature. The adrenal glands, located just above each kidney, release hormones during times of stress. These hormones make a person more alert and increase breathing and heart rate.

During puberty, the hypothalamus and the pituitary glands stimulate the body to grow and develop. They release hormones that stimulate the ovaries in girls to release estrogen and the testes in boys to release testosterone. They also stimulate the ovaries and adrenal glands to produce small amounts of testosterone in girls, and they stimulate the production of small amounts of estrogen in boys. Scientists are not sure why, but in both boys and girls, testosterone and other androgens, or male sex hormones, can stimulate the sebaceous glands to produce more sebum. Boys produce about 10 times more testosterone than girls do, so boys are more likely to develop acne as teenagers. However, because girls often reach puberty before boys, girls with acne are likely to develop it earlier than boys.

The sebaceous glands are sensitive to testosterone and other hormones that are classified as androgens for a reason. The skin cells, hair follicles, and sebaceous glands contain androgen receptors—places that can easily bind with androgens in the bloodstream. Androgens do a lot of good for the skin. They help the skin cells grow and divide so skin cells can replace themselves more quickly. They also help hair grow and become thick. (Men have more body hair than women because androgens bind with androgen receptors in their skin and cause more hair to grow.) Stimulating the sebaceous glands is good for the skin in some ways, because the sebum that is produced moisturizes the skin and protects it. However, when the sebaceous

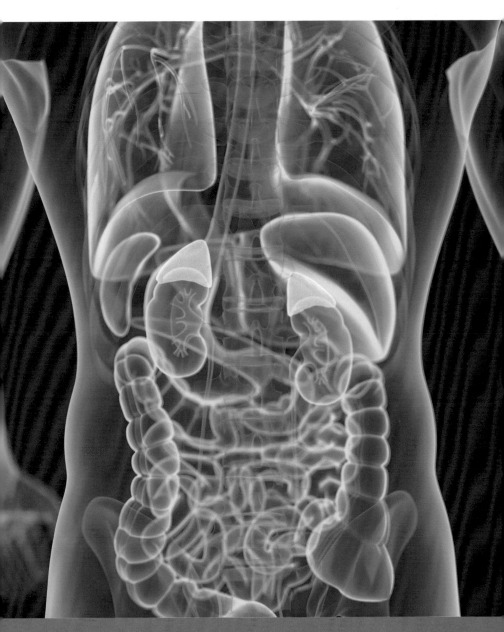

The chemicals released by the adrenal glands (highlighted here) play a role in the formation of acne.

glands are stimulated too much, they can produce too much sebum—and acne is the result.

Once hormone levels increase, whether they do so because of puberty, pregnancy, stress, or for some other reason, sebum levels go up as well. By increasing sebum and by slowing the body's ability to repair its own tissue, hormones set into motion a series of events that can lead to the formation of comedones. Before acne can become red and swollen, though, something else has to happen—the comedone must be infected by the bacterium *P. acnes*.

P. acnes can survive and thrive only in places where there is no oxygen. It lives deep in the skin, where it feeds on sebum. When hormones cause the sebaceous glands to produce more than the usual amount of sebum, it is easy for *P. acnes* populations to swell. As bacterial populations get out of control, the body's immune system responds. White blood cells flock to the area to fight the bacteria. At this point, the comedone may begin to swell, turn red, and feel tender and warm.

PCOS and Acne

Sometimes acne turns out to be just one symptom of an underlying disorder. Adult women who have severe acne may need to be evaluated for polycystic ovary syndrome (PCOS), especially if they are obese and have thinning hair, both of which are also symptoms. They may also have some pelvic pain and patches of thick or dark skin. In polycystic ovary syndrome, the ovaries—and sometimes the adrenal glands—produce a higher-than-normal level of androgens. This interferes with the development and release of eggs by the ovaries. As a result, multiple fluid-filled sacs or cysts can develop on the ovaries. That is why the syndrome is called polycystic. ("Poly" is a term that means "many.")

Women with PCOS may not be able to have children. Most of the time, their ovaries do not release eggs for fertilization. Instead, the ovarian follicles that hold the eggs bunch together and form cysts on the sides of the ovaries. The eggs remain in the cysts and are not released. This makes it difficult or impossible to get pregnant. It can also cause women to have very irregular menstrual cycles. They may not have normal menstrual periods at all. Women with PCOS are often prescribed birth control pills to regulate their menstrual cycle and treat their acne, since their outbreaks are generally tied to the hormonal changes around their period.

The Role of the Immune System

The causes of eczema and psoriasis are less understood than the cause of acne. Researchers believe that for both conditions, the answer has to do with some combination of genes and an environmental trigger. Additionally, both involve the immune system.

People with the most common form of eczema, which is called atopic dermatitis, often have allergies or asthma as well, which are also disorders related to the immune system. Both happen when the immune system is oversensitive to a normal substance and attacks it as a threat. Atopic dermatitis can look similar to an allergic reaction, but it is not the same thing because it is not happening in response to an outside substance. In contrast, allergic contact dermatitis is an allergic reaction; it is eczema that happens when someone touches something they are allergic to. For instance, someone who is allergic to a metal called nickel may get allergic contact dermatitis if they wear nickel jewelry. (American five-cent coins are called nickels because they are made with a combination of this metal and copper.)

Having atopic dermatitis is a strong indicator that someone will also develop a food allergy. According to dermatologist Jon M. Hanifin, "Six to 10 percent of children have atopic dermatitis and ... up to one-third of those individuals may have [a] documented food allergy ... In most cases, patients experience atopic dermatitis before food allergies."[10] They may also develop allergies to things that can be inhaled, such as pollen and pet dander.

According to the National Eczema Association (NEA), recent research suggests that the problem starts with a genetic skin defect that increases the risk of both eczema and allergies. The organization explained,

> *The most commonly reported skin barrier protein defect is a filaggrin gene mutation and this increases the risk of eczema. This skin barrier defect allows allergens to enter through the skin. A number of excellent genetic studies have shown that if this skin barrier protein defect is present, there also exists a greater risk of developing peanut allergy and atopic dermatitis.*[11]

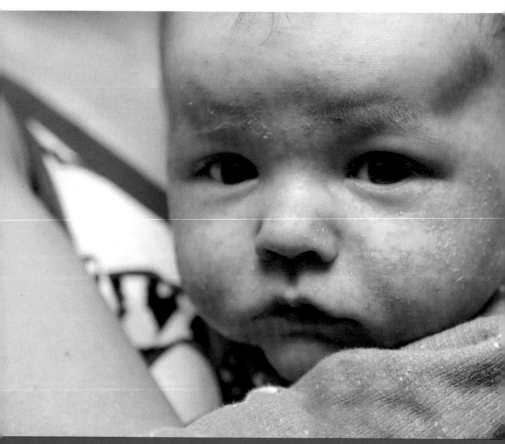

Many babies develop eczema. This is a strong indicator that they will develop food allergies, too.

In other words, while one does not seem to cause the other, allergies and eczema do appear to be linked.

Psoriasis is also linked to the immune system, although not to allergies. In people with psoriasis, the immune system is overactive, which creates inflammation in the body. Inflammation is the visible symptoms of the body's immune response, as white blood cells attack the foreign invader (or what they believe to be a foreign invader). It includes redness, swelling, and heat. With psoriasis, the body attacks its own skin cells, killing them and creating new ones faster than normal. This has two effects. First, it causes the dead skin cells to pile up on the surface of the skin. Second, it creates inflammation. On the surface of the skin, the inflammation is visible. This is what makes the skin red, itchy, and painful. Inside the body, inflammation is invisible, but it can have other effects. One of these is a condition called psoriatic arthritis, which affects 10 to 30 percent of people who have psoriasis. It causes pain and stiffness in inflamed joints.

There are five types of psoriatic arthritis:

- symmetric psoriatic arthritis, which affects the same joints on different sides of the body (for example, both knees) and is similar to rheumatoid arthritis, another autoimmune disorder that causes joint inflammation

- asymmetric psoriatic arthritis, which affects one to three joints at random in the body (for instance, one knee and two fingers)

- distal interphalangeal predominant (DIP) psoriatic arthritis, which mainly affects the joints in the fingers and toes that are closest to the nail and has similar symptoms to osteoarthritis—a condition that occurs when the cartilage around the joints wears away and the bones rub together

- spondylitis, which affects the spinal column, including the neck, lower back, bones of the spine, and pelvic area, as well as connective tissue such as ligaments
- arthritis mutilans, which is a rare but "severe, deforming, and destructive form of psoriatic arthritis that primarily affects the small joints in the fingers and toes closest to the nail. This leads to lost function of the involved joints. It also is frequently associated with lower back and neck pain."[12]

Although experts are aware that eczema and psoriasis are connected to the immune system, they are still not completely sure of the causes. They are aware, however, that certain factors can trigger outbreaks.

Outbreak Triggers

Many people with acne believe their breakouts are not caused by hormones, but by a different factor: stress. Dermatologists agree that stress can cause acne, but stress is not unrelated to the body's hormone levels. Stress dramatically affects the functioning of the hypothalamus and pituitary glands in the brain. Stress also affects members of both sexes by stimulating the adrenal glands to release two other hormones: adrenaline and cortisol. These hormones can make the skin more susceptible to acne in two ways. First, when adrenaline is released, so are androgens. These androgens can bind with the androgen receptors on the sebaceous glands and stimulate the production of more sebum.

Adrenaline and cortisol also suppress the body's immune system. The body becomes less able to fight off infection, so bacteria are more likely to succeed in infecting comedones. The body also becomes slower at healing wounds, so acne lesions

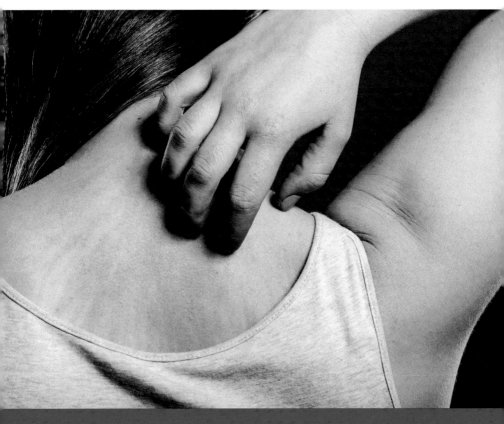

Skin with eczema or psoriasis is generally itchy, but scratching only makes the symptoms worse.

heal more slowly than they otherwise would.

Stress can be a trigger of both eczema and psoriasis as well, although the reasons why are less clear. Scratching the skin is another. In both conditions, the skin is often inflamed and itchy, which naturally makes people want to scratch it. However, scratching does not soothe the itch and only makes the skin damage worse. In the case of eczema, "some people think you have the itching sensation first, then do all the damage to the skin with the scratching and picking, which leads to the rash,"[13] according to dermatologist Whitney High. A pattern known as the itch-scratch cycle can occur: Someone scratches their skin, which makes the condition worse and

Vitiligo

Another autoimmune disorder without a clear cause is called vitiligo. Symptoms appear when the skin cells that produce melanin—the substance that gives skin its color—die or stop working. Experts do not know why this happens; the current theories are that it is a combination of genetics, the immune system attacking the melanin-producing cells, and some kind of trigger such as stress. People with vitiligo are also at an increased risk for skin cancer, eye problems, and hearing loss.

Vitiligo affects all races, but it is especially noticeable in people with darker skin. This can make people feel embarrassed or ashamed, and many people choose to cover their vitiligo with makeup or get treatment that can make it less noticeable. However, others embrace the condition as something that makes them unique. Ash Soto, who developed vitiligo when she was 12, started posting pictures of herself on Instagram when she was 21. She thought she would get negative comments, but instead, she received messages of love and support. The photos and her captions—including statements such as "It's like having natural tie-dye" and "Sometimes I think my vitiligo is painted on like a map from another dimension"[1]—have been a source of inspiration to others who have vitiligo. Soto says she has learned to love herself as she is and hopes she can help others do the same.

Shown here is Winnie Harlow, a fashion model who has vitiligo.

1. Quoted in Lindsey Lanquist, "How Instagram Helped One Woman Fall in Love with Her Vitiligo," *Self*, December 16, 2016. www.self.com/story/vitiligo-instagram.

increases inflammation, which makes the skin itchier, which makes people scratch more.

Other psoriasis triggers include injury to the skin, such as cuts and sunburns, certain medications, heavy alcohol use, and infection. In fact, most cases of guttate psoriasis, which mainly affects young adults and children, are triggered by an infection such as strep throat. When the body has an infection, the immune system goes into overdrive trying to fight it off, which also increases its attacks on its own skin.

Many eczema triggers involve things that irritate the skin by rubbing it or drying it out. They include scented laundry detergent and soap, itchy clothing such as wool sweaters, very hot or very cold weather, and prolonged exposure to water. Eczema patients are advised to moisturize their skin twice a day with a fragrance-free lotion to prevent it from getting too dry. Rarely, a flare-up may also be caused by eating specific foods.

The Role of Genetics

Some acne is thought to be genetic. People are most likely to get it if one or both of their parents had it. A genetic tendency to develop acne could affect a person in various ways. A person might have a genetic tendency to produce more androgens or might simply be more sensitive to them. A person might also have a genetic tendency to heal slowly from wounds or to become infected easily. Understanding why a patient is especially susceptible to acne is important because it can affect the choice of treatment. Hormonal imbalances may be treated one way, while bacterial infections are treated differently.

Understanding the genetic causes of psoriasis and eczema can also help improve treatment. Research in this area is ongoing. It was not until 2017 that researchers identified a gene mutation that is linked to eczema. The gene, called CARD11, "encodes the instructions for producing the CARD11 protein, which has a key role in lymphocyte receptor signaling."[14] In other words, the protein tells white blood cells called lymphocytes what to attack. When multiple health problems occur together, they are called comorbidities. However, researchers found that a CARD11 mutation can cause eczema without causing comorbidities, although some people with eczema do still have them. This is unusual because most autoimmune disorders cause comorbidities. Further research must be done, but knowing which gene is causing the problem and how is a big step toward creating treatments that work more effectively.

Scientists have also done genetic research into psoriasis. They have identified about 25 genetic variants that make someone more likely to develop the disease, although some people who have one or more of these variants never get it at all. The National Psoriasis Foundation explained,

> Scientists now believe that at least 10 percent of the general population inherits one or more of the genes that create a predisposition to psoriasis. However, only two percent to three percent of the population develops the disease. This is thought to be because only two percent to three percent of people encounter the "right" mix of genetics and are exposed to triggers that lead to the development of psoriasis.[15]

Anne Bowcock, a professor of genetics at Washington University School of Medicine in St. Louis, has identified one specific gene mutation that leads to plaque psoriasis when it is activated by an environmental trigger, such as an infection. This mutation, called CARD14, has also been linked to pustular psoriasis and psoriatic arthritis. As of 2018, it is the only gene mutation directly linked to psoriasis; the factors that determine whether the other genetic variants will cause the disease are still unknown. As with the genetic eczema research, this information will likely lead to new and improved treatments.

CHAPTER THREE

TREATMENT FOR COMMON CONDITIONS

Some people's skin condition is mild enough that they can treat it at home with products that can be bought in any drugstore, such as moisturizer or a medicated face wash. These products generally take some time to work, so results may not be seen until after the person has been using them once or twice a day for several weeks. However, if the skin is not responsive after a few months, if the condition seems to be quickly getting worse, or if there are wounds that will not heal, the person should make an appointment with a dermatologist for a diagnosis, prescriptions, and advice.

Myths About Acne

There are many myths about acne causes and treatment. One is that it is caused because someone does not wash their face enough. *P. acnes* is located deep within the skin, not at the surface. This means that although washing and exfoliating with mild cleansers is good for the skin, too much washing can actually irritate and infect whiteheads and blackheads, causing more pimples. Many people react to new breakouts by scrubbing their skin clean several times a day with harsh cleansers. Dermatologists caution that this is probably one of the worst things one can do. "Acne is rarely the result of poor hygiene," said dermatologist

Richard Fried. "Attempts to clean or even sterilize the skin often cause more problems than they solve."[16] Products such as sunscreen and moisturizer are also important, but many contain oil, so people whose skin is prone to acne should make sure to buy products labeled "noncomedogenic," which means non-pore clogging.

Different products containing salicylic acid can be used to treat warts (shown here) and acne. They can often be purchased at a drugstore.

Another myth is that putting toothpaste on a pimple will clear it up quickly. According to dermatologist Rebecca Baxt, "Toothpaste irritates the skin, so some may believe that it dries out pimples, but what it really does is irritate and cause redness and peeling."[17] It is more effective and better for the skin to use a gentle cleanser. Some acne products contain benzoyl peroxide, which kills *P. acnes* and heals pimples, or salicylic acid, which is an exfoliant and an anti-inflammatory agent. However, dermatologist Marianne O'Donoghue warned,

> *If you are using a benzoyl peroxide or salicylic acid soap all over your face, that area under the eye where the skin is so thin and tender can get really sore and irritated. I would rather see a patient use Dove on her whole face and then put the acne medicines just where she needs them. Also, while it may be okay to use an acne soap with an over the counter acne lotion, if you are using an acne soap with a prescription acne treatment, you can end up being chapped and unable to use the prescription where you need it.*[18]

Acne-Like Breakouts

Some makeup can cause an acneiform eruption—an outbreak of spots that look like acne but are not technically acne, since they are not caused by an overproduction of sebum. These spots are called acne cosmetica. If spots appear overnight, though, they are not acne cosmetica, but a different condition: chemical folliculitis. Folliculitis occurs when follicles in the skin become red, inflamed, and irritated. When folliculitis is caused by a reaction to chemicals, such as the chemicals in cosmetics, it is called chemical folliculitis. When chemical folliculitis develops, the cure is to stop using the product that produced the reaction.

Another type of disorder that is often confused with acne is rosacea—specifically subtype two, papulopustular rosacea, which causes small, pus-filled bumps to appear on the nose, cheeks, and forehead. Subtype one, erythematotelangiectatic rosacea, causes redness and dry, scaly, burning skin, which may be confused with eczema; however, it only appears on the face. The causes of rosacea are unknown, although some things are known to make breakouts worse, including spicy food, alcohol, and an infection with the intestinal bacterium *Helicobacter pylori*, which also causes ulcers (holes in the intestinal wall). There is no cure for rosacea, although it can be treated with a dermatologist-recommended skin care routine. Rosacea patients are advised to avoid direct sunlight as well as skin products that contain alcohol, menthol, witch hazel, or exfoliants.

Everyone's skin is different, and someone may need to experiment with several different treatments before they find the one that works best for them.

A third acne myth is that exposure to sunlight clears up pimples. However, while some sunlight may temporarily clear up breakouts, some doctors feel that sunlight stimulates the sebaceous glands. "In my practice, the busiest time of year for acne is October," said New York dermatologist Laurie Polis. "People go out in the sun in the summer; the sunlight stimulates the follicles. And a few months later, you've got more acne."[19] Additionally, long-term exposure to the sun without some kind of protection, such as sunscreen or a hat, can dry out skin and increase the risk of skin cancer.

Talking to a Dermatologist

When acne first begins, many people try to treat it themselves. However, over-the-counter (OTC) remedies can be expensive, especially if they do not work. Severe acne may cause someone to avoid going out when they do not have to, but avoiding social engagements can be hard on a teen's self-esteem, and skipping school can be hard on a teen's academic record. When self-treatment and OTC treatments do not help, it may be time to see a doctor. "It's a personal choice," said dermatologist Kent Taulbee. "We see people at all stages. I think if it's becoming a problem socially, you're worried about long-term scarring and it's interfering with your lifestyle and self-esteem, it's time to see me."[20]

People should also see a dermatologist if they are not sure whether the condition they have is acne or something else. Eruptions that look like acne pimples may actually be rosacea, contact dermatitis, pustular psoriasis, or in rare cases, even skin cancer. It is also important to see a specialist if acne appears in an unusual location, such as an armpit. Additionally, people who know they have other skin disorders should discuss their acne with a dermatologist because treating two skin conditions at the same time can be tricky.

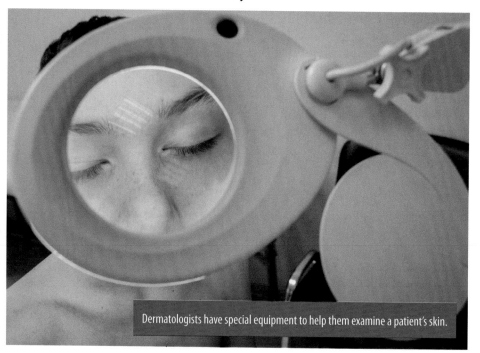

Dermatologists have special equipment to help them examine a patient's skin.

A dermatologist will begin the diagnosis of acne in much the same way an acne sufferer would at home—by looking at the skin in good light. Dermatologists can check to see if the acne is deep or just on the surface, if it is infected, and whether or not there is scarring or skin discoloration. In some cases, a dermatologist will order a blood test to rule out another disorder.

Once the diagnosis of acne has been confirmed, the next step is to identify the cause and treat it. Dermatologists can treat acne at any point in its development—by attacking the bacteria that can cause an infection, by opening the pores and reducing the likelihood that a comedone will form and plug a hair follicle, or by trying to adjust the balance of hormones in the body that can cause sebum production to increase in the first place.

Acne Prescriptions

When dermatologists suspect that acne is being caused by an overgrowth of bacteria, they often prescribe an antibiotic—a drug that kills bacteria. Antibiotics can be taken orally, or they can be applied to the acne in the form of a cream. (Most over-the-counter acne creams also contain ingredients such as benzoyl peroxide that are meant to kill bacteria.) In the case of his patient Susan, Fried prescribed both. He said,

> *I asked that she abandon (at least temporarily) her over-the-counter products and use only the products I recommended. I prescribed a brief course of antibiotics combined with topical medications. The regimen was clear and simple, and it allowed Susan to wear whatever makeup she desired. Her skin responded quickly.*[21]

Not only did Susan's acne improve, but over time, it went away entirely. It is not generally a good idea for an acne patient to stay on antibiotics forever, though. "I believe that you should always be looking for an exit strategy,"[22] said Fried. He was able to convince Susan to take steps to reduce her stress levels. She began to spend less time working and more time pursuing her social life and hobbies, and she was able to discontinue her antibiotic treatment.

Why is it so important for Susan and other acne patients to minimize the amount of time they spend taking antibiotic drugs? Antibiotics have side effects, including increasing a person's sensitivity to the sun and upsetting the gastrointestinal tract. Antibiotics kill bacteria, but the body relies on its bacterial balance to stay well. People on antibiotics are more at risk for yeast infections as a result. In addition, any time a person takes antibiotics, there is a danger that antibiotic-resistant bacteria may evolve. Antibiotic-resistant bacteria are bacteria that cannot be killed with any of the commonly used antibiotics, which makes treatment difficult or impossible in the future.

Not all acne is infected with bacteria, however. For some patients, antibiotic treatment does little good. For patients who have blackheads and whiteheads that do not tend to get infected, many dermatologists prefer to begin by prescribing a retinoid. Retinoids such as Retin-A, or tretinoin, are medicines that come from vitamin A. They work by reducing the formation of microcomedones—the little plugs of dead skin cells that block the pores and cause acne to develop—and by keeping the pores open. By stopping the formation of microcomedones, retinoids can prevent acne from forming. They also treat acne that has already developed by reducing inflammation. This means that pimples and cysts that have already formed may start to shrink and may become less red. Because retinoids both prevent acne and treat current flare-ups, they can be very effective at clearing the skin.

Retinoids have some side effects, however. The most common are dry skin and chapping. Retinoids can also cause redness and inflammation that is similar to a sunburn. The skin may also become very sensitive to sunlight. Patients who use retinoids must commit to using sunscreen regularly to protect their skin. "The medicines I tried really dried out my skin," commented actress Chrishell Stause after her first few visits to a dermatologist. "Sometimes it was painful and I became very sensitive to the sun … The medicines basically took away one problem, but added more."[23]

A retinoid gel can also be used to treat psoriasis,

but it generally makes eczema worse. This is one of the few treatments that is not recommended for both diseases.

A Powerful Drug

Dermatologists say that one retinoid—isotretinoin, commonly known as Roaccutane—is the most powerful acne drug they have ever found. It helps the cells inside hair follicles become normal, reduces sebum production, and reduces inflammation, making cystic acne less red and swollen. It has an 80 percent success rate if taken for about five months, but it is so powerful that it is only prescribed for severe acne that does not respond to other treatments.

Although isotretinoin works, it has some severe and sometimes dangerous side effects. Because it reduces sebum production, it often makes skin incredibly dry. In an article for *The Atlantic*, former acne patient Emily Goldberg wrote, "A light touch was all it took for the skin on my forehead to come off in flakes, and thin layers peeled off like an onion. Chapstick became a constant necessity."[1] Pregnant women cannot take it, as it causes serious birth defects. Additionally, isotretinoin has been linked to an increased risk of depression, suicidal thoughts, and other psychiatric disorders.

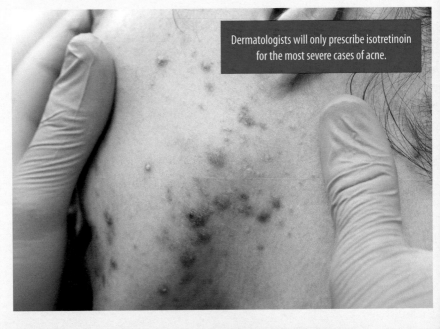

Dermatologists will only prescribe isotretinoin for the most severe cases of acne.

1. Emily Goldberg, "The Scorched-Earth Acne Solution," *The Atlantic*, February 13, 2017. www.theatlantic.com/health/archive/2017/02/accutane-acne-drug-side-effects/516345/.

Treating Eczema and Psoriasis

Eczema and psoriasis are not curable, but there are treatments that can address the symptoms of these diseases and keep them under control. The first step is for a person to figure out their triggers. These can be different for everyone. Some, such as an infection, sweating too much, or hormonal changes—especially for women, as their hormones change during their menstrual cycle—can be difficult to avoid. However, it is better to know what they are so the person can be prepared to treat an outbreak.

There are several types of treatments available for eczema and psoriasis. OTC skin-care products can be bought in many stores. According to the NEA, "Some OTC eczema treatments are used for moisturizing skin; some are used to help skin symptoms such as rash, redness and itch; and some are for gently cleaning skin to prevent infection."[24] Most eczema treatments can also be used for

Petroleum jelly is an example of an ointment. Ointments have the highest oil content compared to creams and lotions, so they work the best at keeping skin with eczema from drying out.

psoriasis. For instance, coal tar creams and shampoos can be found in many drugstores. These products reduce itchiness caused by inflammation.

Moisturizing is especially important for people with eczema or psoriasis, since dry skin is a common trigger. Wind, cold air, certain cleaning products, and washing too often are all things that can dry the skin out. Not all moisturizers are good for people with these diseases. For instance, a scented moisturizer may dry skin out more due to the chemicals used to make the scent. Experts recommend using a moisturizer that contains a lot of oil, such as an ointment (as opposed to a cream or a lotion), because those are best at locking moisture into the skin. If a product has the NEA or National Psoriasis Foundation (NPF) seal on it, it means these organizations think it is one of the best products for someone with eczema or psoriasis to use.

Moisturizers are most effective when applied right after a bath. This is because dry skin does not retain enough water. Experts recommend taking at least one bath or shower per day. Some people add certain things to their baths to increase moisturization or decrease symptoms such as redness and itching. These include bath oils, baking soda, a half-cup of bleach (diluted bleach is believed to decrease inflammation and kill infection-causing bacteria on the skin), oatmeal, salt, or vinegar. Each person is different, however, so what works for one person may not work for another.

There are some special modifications people with eczema or psoriasis need to make to their bathing routine. While many people take a bath or shower in hot water, this can make dry skin worse in the long term—so can exposure to water, which is why experts recommend the following steps in the "soak and seal" method to let the water be absorbed instead of evaporating and drying out the skin:

- *Take a bath using lukewarm (not hot) water for five to 10 minutes. Use a gentle cleanser (no soaps) and avoid scrubbing the affected skin.*
- *After bathing, pat the skin lightly with a towel, leaving it slightly damp.*
- *Apply prescription topical medication to the affected areas of skin as directed.*
- *Within three minutes, liberally apply a moisturizer all over the body. It's important to apply the moisturizer within three minutes or the skin may become even drier.*
- *Wait a few minutes to let the moisturizer absorb into the skin before dressing or applying wet wraps.*[25]

A wet wrap is, as the name suggests, a wet cloth that is wrapped around an area affected by eczema. It can be applied at home unless the affected area is on the face, in which case it must be applied by a specially trained nurse. Wet wraps are mainly used to treat eczema symptoms, but some psoriasis patients may also find that they help. To do wet wrap therapy, the person first needs clean cotton clothing or gauze, which they run under warm water until it is slightly damp. They wrap the damp cloth around the area that has eczema, then they place a dry layer of cloth over it. If the eczema is on the hands or feet, they can use gloves, cotton socks, or plastic wrap for the dry layer. Finally, they dress in clothes such as pajamas or a sweatshirt and sweatpants, taking care not to disturb the two layers of their wrap. Wet wraps are most effective when worn for several hours or overnight.

According to the NEA, "Moisturizing is one of the most effective treatments, but it's only able to control the mildest forms of eczema when used on its own."[26] The same is true of psoriasis. In many cases, something stronger is needed.

Topical Treatments

Products that can be applied to the skin (rather than taken as a pill or injected) are called topicals. Many people first try to control their eczema or psoriasis with OTC topicals, but if those do not work, a dermatologist can prescribe a stronger topical.

There are several different kinds of prescription topicals available. Corticosteroid creams—often shortened to just "steroid creams"—are one of the products most commonly prescribed to treat eczema and psoriasis. Steroids occur naturally in the body; they are substances that regulate growth and immune function. They can be copied in a lab and used in medication to help boost these functions and to suppress inflammation. Corticosteroids are different than anabolic steroids, which build muscle and are sometimes used by athletes against the rules of their sports. There

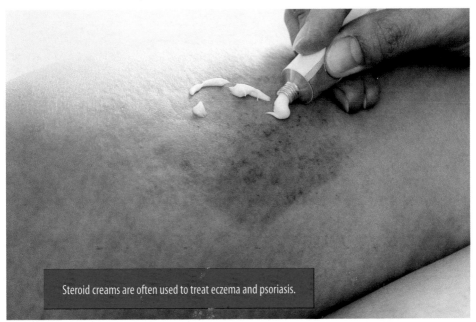

Steroid creams are often used to treat eczema and psoriasis.

are seven different classes of steroids. They range from Class 7 (least potent) to Class 1 (superpotent). The class a person is prescribed depends on how severe their symptoms are.

Because steroids are strong medication, they can have some severe side effects. These include thinning or thickening of the skin where they are applied, stretch marks, and darkening of the skin. Less commonly, they may cause eye damage, acne, or suppression of the adrenal glands. For this reason, doctors say someone should use only the recommended amount and should stop using it once the inflammation is under control. If it comes back again, they can start using the medication again, but they should not use it while their skin is clear.

Topical calcineurin inhibitors (TCIs) are a second type of prescription treatment. Once they are absorbed into the skin, they "work by stopping a piece of the immune system from 'switching on,' preventing it from causing ... symptoms such as redness and itch."[27] Because they do not contain steroids, they can be used even on delicate skin such as the eyelids, and the only side effect is a mild burning or stinging feeling when the medicine is first applied, which fades quickly. TCIs may cause the skin to become more sensitive to light, so people should take care to cover the affected skin when they go out in the sun. They can also increase the risk of skin cancer, so they are not recommended for long-term or continuous use.

A third type of prescription topical is called a PDE4 inhibitor. It works by stopping an enzyme called phosphodiesterase 4 (PDE4) from creating inflammation in the body. The NEA explained,

> PDE4 is produced by cells in our immune system and helps the body function in part by controlling cytokines. Cytokines are bits of protein

also produced by our cells that contribute to inflammation. When cytokines are mistakenly triggered in the body, the resulting inflammation can contribute to the development of certain diseases, including atopic dermatitis.[28]

As of 2018, there is only one PDE4 inhibitor approved by the U.S. Food and Drug Administration (FDA) for eczema. It is called Eucrisa, and in clinical trials—tests of a new drug or treatment on human participants to make sure it is safe and effective—participants noticed nearly or completely clear skin after using it for 28 days. Its most commonly reported side effect is irritation on the skin where it is applied. Eucrisa is currently being tested to see if it works for psoriasis.

Phototherapy

Another form of treatment that focuses on the area of skin affected by eczema or psoriasis is called phototherapy. Phototherapy uses a special light that mimics sunlight—most commonly, ultraviolet B (UVB), one of the types of rays the sun gives off—to reduce itchiness and inflammation while increasing the body's production of vitamin D and the skin's bacteria-fighting abilities. It is generally prescribed after topical treatments have failed. The NEA described a typical phototherapy session:

- *During your visit you will apply a moisturizing oil to the skin and stand in the cabinet undressed except for underwear and goggles to protect the eyes.*

- *The machine will be activated for a short time, usually just seconds to minutes, and will treat the entire body, or just certain exposed areas.*

- *Careful records are kept of your response and the light is slowly increased with each treatment.*[29]

At first, patients generally have sessions nearly every day. If they respond well to the treatment after several months—which about 70 percent do—they can reduce it to once or twice a week. If their symptoms disappear entirely, they can stop treatment for a while to see if they will stay away. People who take medications that make their skin sensitive to light, such as TCIs, should stop using that medication while receiving phototherapy.

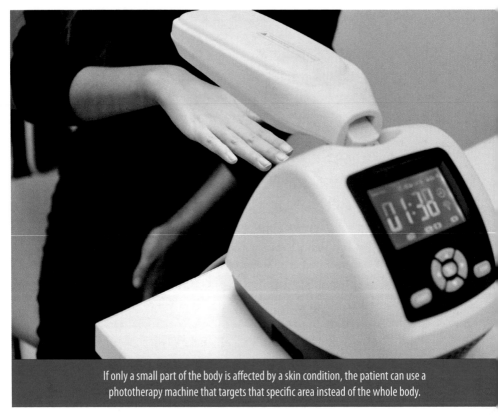

If only a small part of the body is affected by a skin condition, the patient can use a phototherapy machine that targets that specific area instead of the whole body.

Although phototherapy can have good results, it can also cause some dangerous complications. Because UVB rays are a form of radiation, too much exposure can damage skin cells, leading to mild side effects, such as sunburn, or severe ones, such as a deadly form of skin cancer called melanoma. Additionally, if someone does not wear their goggles properly during treatment, they can experience eye damage. Fortunately, these risks are minimal because people are treated under the supervision of medical experts who typically know the amount of exposure needed to treat eczema and psoriasis without causing negative effects. For this reason, phototherapy is generally considered a safe treatment.

Systemic Treatments

In addition to a topical treatment, a dermatologist may prescribe medications that are taken orally (by mouth) or intravenously (by injection). These are called systemic treatments. A systemic treatment is one that spreads throughout the whole body rather than being confined to the specific area where the symptoms appear, the way topical treatments are. Systemic treatments include immunosuppressants, oral retinoids, and oral corticosteroids. They generally work quickly and effectively, but they can have some severe side effects.

Immunosuppressants, as the name implies, suppress the immune system to decrease the body's inflammation response. They can be given either orally or intravenously. They are not the first line of treatment because, by suppressing the immune system, they increase a person's risk of getting sick, as it becomes harder for the body to fight off real invaders. The other two systemic treatments also have more severe side effects and are considered a last resort. For instance, oral retinoids can cause high cholesterol, decreased thyroid function, and sensitivity to the sun. Oral steroids can cause weight gain, a decrease in bone density, and mood changes. They can also suppress the immune system, although that is not their main function. According to Professor Andrew Wright, consultant dermatologist at St. Luke's Hospital in Bradford, England, "Systemic treatments are recommended for adults and children with severe eczema who are troubled with repeated, widespread flare-ups of the disease, or who have eczema that is hard to control with topical treatments alone."[30] The same is true of psoriasis. The only systemic treatment that is currently approved for people between the ages of 2 and 18 is an immunosuppressant called ciclosporin.

Sometimes young adults with severe eczema or psoriasis that does not respond to other treatments are given oral steroids, but this is considered a short-term treatment because of the way the medicine can interfere with bone growth. Young adults who are prescribed a systemic treatment are closely watched by medical professionals to make sure they are not experiencing dangerous side effects.

Many treatments for eczema and psoriasis are similar because they are both inflammatory diseases that make the skin itchy and red. However, some treatments are specifically targeted to slow down cell growth, which happens only with psoriasis, not eczema. One systemic treatment specifically for psoriasis is methotrexate, which was originally developed to treat cancer. According to the NPF, "In a person with psoriasis, methotrexate binds to and inhibits an enzyme involved in the rapid growth of skin cells and slows down their growth rate."[31] Although it can be effective at treating psoriasis, it can have serious complications, especially concerning the liver. People who take this medication must have regular blood tests to make sure their liver is not being damaged by it.

Other psoriasis treatments include:

• synthetic, or manmade, versions of vitamin D
• anthralin, a topical treatment
• Goeckerman therapy, which uses phototherapy

and coal tar together to increase the skin's receptiveness to UVB rays
- excimer laser, a form of light therapy that uses a beam of more powerful UVB light to target psoriasis plaques only

Managing Stress

Alternative treatments are ones that are not generally used in Western medical practices. They include herbal remedies, acupuncture, and yoga. However, in recent years, alternative medical practices have become more accepted in the Western medical community. Some doctors are integrating alternative medicine into their practices. When they do this, the treatments are called complementary because they are working with Western medical treatments.

Alternative practitioners are doctors who reccomend non-drug treatments only. They try to

One alternative treatment is aromatherapy, which involves scents that are believed to be relaxing. While aromatherapy will not cure a skin condition, it may help relieve stress, which can cut down on outbreaks.

work with a patient to make changes to diet and life-style, emphasizing sleep, exercise, and good nutrition. They also emphasize using natural methods, such as yoga and meditation, to keep stress levels low. When medical intervention is needed, alternative practitioners tend to recommend natural remedies. They regard drug treatment as a last resort. Alternative treatments alone generally cannot cure a disease, but they can help improve the effectiveness of other treatments.

Acne, psoriasis, eczema, and other skin conditions can all be made worse by stress. According to alternative health educator Billie Sahley, "Anger, depression, anxiety, and fear all cause measurable skin changes, including shifts in blood flow, moisture, and temperature."[32] Many alternative practitioners suggest that skin disorder patients who have high stress levels make more time to do things that they find relaxing. This could mean taking time to pursue a favorite hobby, such as gardening, exercising, or knitting. It could also mean taking time to get more sleep or meditate once or twice a day.

Many doctors recommend guided imagery to help people relax. Guided imagery is a process that patients can use to relax, let go of stress, and help their bodies heal. "After 40 years of medical practice, I find guided imagery the easiest way for people to relax," explained family doctor Martin Rossman. "The simplest thing is to daydream yourself to a safe place of stresslessness." As a way of practicing guided imagery, Rossman encourages patients to relive, in their memory, the best experience of their lives. "They can do that in a fraction of a second," he said. "They can see what the day was like, what was said, the experience. It's multisensory. Imagery allows you to get that whole experience."[33]

Rossman explained that worry is also a form of

guided imagery, but it is a negative form. When people worry all the time, they put their body into a perpetual state of alarm. "When the mind is full of worries," he says, "and you go over them day and night, your brain is constantly sending messages down through the autonomic nervous system to keep the body in an alarm state."[34] Staying in an alarm state means that the body releases the hormones adrenaline and cortisol into the bloodstream to cope with the added stress. Both of these hormones can stimulate the sebaceous glands. They can also depress the immune system so that if pimples and cysts form, they will not heal very quickly.

Natural Remedies

Some non-drug treatments for certain skin conditions do not have scientific evidence behind them, but many patients report that they work. Many relieve itching and inflammation, and some help control bacteria. Some treatments are applied to the skin, while others are taken in pill or powder form. All treatments should be discussed with a doctor before they are tried, especially when combining multiple ingredients. The most commonly recommended natural remedies include:

- tea tree oil
- witch hazel
- turmeric
- chamomile
- manjistha
- neem
- oat paste or an oat bath
- Oregon grape
- aloe vera
- apple cider vinegar
- capsaicin
- Dead Sea salts or Epsom salts
- sunflower or coconut oil
- cardiospermum
- topical vitamin B12

Some alternative practitioners believe that patients can use the brain's ability to visualize—in other words, their imagination—to increase blood flow on purpose to certain parts of the body, including the skin, helping those areas to heal. Others, including many Western psychologists and psychotherapists, simply believe that guided imagery is an easy way to help patients relax. Relaxing gives patients who have a skin condition a chance to let their bodies recover from surges of emotional hormones, giving the skin a chance to recover as well.

Improving Diet

Making changes to their diet is another way people with a skin condition can manage their symptoms. The best diet for most skin conditions is an anti-inflammatory one. This means following a diet that is based on whole foods—foods that have not been processed or have been processed only minimally. It also means eating a diet based on fruits and vegetables, with occasional small servings of whole grains. Red meat, sugar, and dairy products should be kept to a minimum in the diet. Instead, people should eat nuts, seeds, and cold-water fish such as salmon.

Fruits and vegetables are important because they are food sources of vitamins and minerals that the body needs in order to repair its cells and grow new cells and tissues. Deficiencies in certain nutrients can trigger an acne outbreak or an attack of psoriasis or eczema. These include omega-3 fatty acids as well as important minerals such as zinc, magnesium, chromium, and selenium, and vitamins A, B, C, and E. Each nutrient serves important functions in the body. Omega-3 fatty acids are helpful for making sure that sebum contains enough linoleic acid to help skin cells slough off the sides of hair follicles efficiently, without getting stuck and forming comedones. Zinc and vitamin A are important in helping the body grow new cells and repair its tissues. Zinc, A and B vitamins, and vitamin C also provide support to the immune system. In addition to controlling eczema and psoriasis outbreaks, having a healthy immune system can help the body avoid bacterial infections so pimples do not become as red and swollen as they otherwise might. People can get extra vitamins and minerals from supplements, but it is also important for them to eat foods that naturally contain those substances. Experts recommend avoiding processed foods because when foods are processed, they lose a lot of their nutritional value. For example, a whole peach will have more vitamins in it than canned peaches.

In addition to providing the body with the nutrients it needs to grow, develop, and repair tissue by encouraging cells to reproduce, food also affects the balance of hormones in the body. Vitamin B6 is thought to reduce the effects of testosterone on the body. The phytochemicals in soybeans have the effect of reducing the amount of testosterone and other androgens in the blood, so the androgen

An anti-inflammatory diet, which includes the foods shown here, has been shown to help some people manage their skin conditions.

receptors in the sebaceous glands are less likely to become overstimulated. Lycopene, a substance that forms in cooked tomatoes, also reduces testosterone in the blood. High-fiber meals also tend to hold down the levels of testosterone in the blood. Green tea helps keep hormone levels stable. In patients who are sensitive to gluten, removing foods such as bread and pasta may also help. However, not everyone has this sensitivity, so individual results vary.

Just as some foods can help balance and control hormones, however, other foods can cause hormones to surge out of control. Sugar, meat, dairy products, and vegetable oils are some of the worst offenders, which is why they are not part of an anti-inflammatory diet. Staying hydrated is also very important. At minimum, experts recommend drinking 64 ounces (2 liters) of water per day, but this number may be higher for certain people depending on their weight and activity level. Drinking water keeps the skin hydrated, which helps it stay healthy. For patients with eczema in

Drinking water is important for overall health, including clearer skin.

particular, doctors recommend drinking mineral water instead of tap water because the minerals in the water help reduce the effects of the disease. Staying hydrated can also help reduce the effects of psoriatic arthritis, and it helps the body get rid of any toxins.

Acne and Sugar

For most of the latter half of the 20th century, dermatologists claimed that there was no connection between diet and acne. In recent years, though, dermatologists such as Richard Fried have come to believe that patients should try to avoid any foods they consider to be personal triggers for their acne. Fried advocates that patients keep a journal in which they record everything they ate each day, how much exercise they got, what products they used on their skin, and how their acne was that day. This way, patients may be able to identify their personal triggers. Anecdotally, dermatologists say that patients often identify sugar as a trigger.

In 2007, Australian researchers decided to study this issue. They were interested in how the position of a food on the glycemic index might affect hormone levels. Foods that are low on the glycemic index (often referred to as low-GI foods) are foods that are digested slowly. They do not cause any sudden spikes in blood sugar. Peanuts, grapefruit, and apples are low-GI foods. High-GI foods, on the other hand, are digested very quickly. They cause blood sugar levels to spike quickly, and sometimes blood sugar will remain high for several hours. Table sugar is a high-GI food, but so are many foods that do not taste sweet, such as baked potatoes, white bread, and white rice.

The Australian researchers had their study subjects focus on eating foods that contained plenty of protein but were low on the glycemic index. After three months, they noticed that blood insulin levels had dropped dramatically in the low-GI group, as compared to the control group, who were not focused on only eating those foods. At the same time, the patients in the low-GI group were pleased to discover that their faces were clearing up and that they were losing weight. Losing weight affected their acne, too, because in women, fat cells produce cortisol and androgens.

While some patients find that changing their diet works wonders for their skin condition, others do not see any noticeable improvement. This can be frustrating for more than one reason. Psoriasis researcher Dr. Joel Gelfland explained, "The downside [of changing your diet] is the time, cost and energy to follow a diet you may not enjoy, and that won't have proven benefits for your health."[35] Some people find that an anti-inflammatory diet improves their overall health but does not clear up their skin condition or only partially clears it up. Trying treatments that do not work is one thing that makes life with a skin condition all the more frustrating.

CHAPTER FOUR

LIVING WITH A SKIN CONDITION

Although there are many effective treatments for skin conditions such as acne, psoriasis, and eczema, there are no surefire cures. Someone may successfully undergo a particular treatment and live for months or years with clear skin, only to later encounter something that triggers a breakout. Additionally, many treatments take some time to work, even if they are eventually effective. For a small percentage of people, treatments do not work at all. For these reasons, people with skin conditions often have to learn to live with the visible symptoms of their illness. For many, a breakout of any type can cause stress and embarrassment. Understanding how someone with a skin condition feels can help their loved ones support them.

Facing Stigma

People with skin conditions often have to deal with stigma, which is a negative view about something. Generally, this stigma comes from misunderstanding the disease. People often think conditions such as eczema and psoriasis are contagious, so they avoid people who have them. This can be hurtful to people who have the disease, especially since they are not contagious at all. People may also look down on someone who has a skin condition if they believe it is a result of poor over-all health. In reality, while making changes in diet, exercise, and stress management may help manage outbreaks, they are not proven cures. A person can be healthy in every other way and still have a skin condition.

The stigma of a skin condition can result in people being treated unfairly. In one example, a woman with eczema named Emily Loh took a trip from Barcelona, Spain, to Paris, France. A blog entry on the website AD RescueWear, which sells special clothing and skin products for eczema sufferers, explained that when Loh showed up for her flight, an airline agent "suggested that Emily should be required to carry a doctor's note confirming that it is safe for her to fly with other passengers ... Emily had just about enough of this treatment at this point, asking if someone with acne or another visible skin condition would be treated this way."[36] The airline later sent her an apology note, but the damage was done; Loh was embarrassed in front of her fellow passengers. Jennie Lyon, the author of the blog entry, offered this advice for eczema sufferers who face similar remarks from teachers, classmates, or friends' parents: "If confronted with this kind of unfair singling out, it is best to keep your cool and try to explain the situation as best you can to the person ... Without becoming visibly upset, make sure that they know how you feel and exactly what the condition is."[37]

Effects on Mental Health

Unfortunately, people with a visible skin condition—even a common one, such as acne—often face teasing and bullying because of their appearance. This can cause embarrassment and social isolation. Daniel Boey, one of the most successful fashion show producers in the world, said that he was mostly unaffected by his eczema until others pointed it out: "I began to take notice of it in primary school, when classmates would point out (and sometimes laugh at) the red patches on my joints after physical education classes. I guess I never noticed them before, and it started to make me really self-conscious."[38] People with a skin condition may stop doing things they enjoy. For example, someone with psoriasis on their back may not go to the beach in the summer because they are too embarrassed to wear a bathing suit. Over time, this embarrassment and isolation often lead to mental health issues such as depression and anxiety. It is also stressful, and increased stress can lead to more breakouts and flare-ups,

Embarrassment about a skin condition can lead to isolation and depression.

which can increase stress even further, leading to a vicious cycle.

People are often advised to just ignore others' opinions, but "that's not realistic for most people. We're all dependent on others. Even the most self-confident among us are affected by how people see us."[39] Sometimes ignoring other people's ignorance of a skin condition is the most helpful course of action, but others times it can be more helpful to educate them about the facts of the disease. People who do not have a skin condition should also make an effort to learn about acne, psoriasis, eczema, and other chronic conditions so they can avoid saying or doing things that are hurtful to someone with one of these disorders.

A large part of the impact skin conditions have on a person's mental health is the emphasis society places on looking attractive—and the narrowness of its definition of "attractive." Magazines, billboards, and commercials show models with flawless skin, and thousands of products are marketed to help people achieve the same clear, glowing skin. Acne ads, in particular, make a point of mentioning how unattractive acne is, which can have a negative impact on how people with acne view themselves and are viewed by others. However, many people do not realize that society's beauty standards are generally set by companies trying to sell products. By convincing people that their skin condition is ugly and having this reinforced by the people around them, the company ensures that people are more likely to buy their products. Additionally, even most models do not have the perfect skin they appear to have. Their imperfections are covered with makeup or Photoshopped out of the final picture. This gives people a false idea of how they "should" look—one that is unachievable for most people. Models and actors who do have perfect skin often spend large amounts of time and money on their skin-care routine, which is also unattainable for the average person.

"Acne teaches us to look for flaws," said Gail Robinson, former president of the American Counseling Association. "That becomes habitual, a way of viewing yourself."[40] Even celebrities with acne find that it affects how they feel about themselves. Tennis star Serena Williams said that acne lowered her self-esteem. "If I'm worrying about my skin, I'm distracted and can't play my best," she said. "It's like having a big spotlight on your face. I felt like 'Oh, God, I'm gonna be on the court and playing in front of millions of people worldwide. Is that photographer gonna snap this volcano on my right cheek?'"[41]

Singer and actress Jessica Simpson had a similar experience with acne around her chin and mouth, as she explained:

> I was on my first tour, and the stress was just amazing. I had a terrible, terrible breakout. I just started looking sad because of the blemishes that I had. And when I shot my videos, they had to go in and digitally fix my chin. It was to the point where I was embarrassed to go on-stage or do photo shoots ... my fans ... were just shocked when they saw me. I wasn't what they saw on the cover of the magazine.[42]

Knowing all of this, however, does not necessarily make someone feel better, especially when the people they interact with reinforce society's beauty standards. If someone feels upset enough by their skin condition to have it affect their daily moods and behaviors, they can talk to a therapist

Celebrities such as Serena Williams (shown here) often feel anxious about the way their skin looks because they are constantly being photographed.

who can help them figure out ways to boost their self-esteem and love themselves just as they are.

When Is It Time to See a Therapist?

Everyone feels dissatisfied with their appearance sometimes; someone may get a haircut they dislike or have an acne breakout the day before school picture day. However, a chronic skin condition—especially one that is difficult to manage or does not respond well to treatment—can lead to serious mental health issues such as depression, anxiety, and even thoughts of suicide. A person should see a therapist if they have some or all of the following symptoms:

- difficulty concentrating at school or work
- feelings of guilt, worthlessness, or hopelessness, especially if they lead to thoughts of suicide
- sleeping too much or too little
- loss of interest in normal activities
- feeling unusually sad or numb

- irritability and restlessness
- panic or fear over normal situations (for example, going out in public)
- shortness of breath, nausea, dizziness, or muscle tension that has been confirmed by a medical doctor to have a psychological rather than physical cause

Overcoming Stigma

Fortunately, the growing body positivity movement has extended to the skin's appearance. For example, when 18-year-old Hailey Wait began posting pictures of herself on Instagram without hiding her acne, she received messages from her followers thanking her for helping them accept their own acne. Experts say it is unlikely that acne will become a desirable trait, but it may change the way products are marketed, which is the goal many want to see achieved. According to Megan Collins, a trend forecaster, "Consumers—Gen Zs, especially—are sick of being told by these huge companies that they need to look a certain way, that they need to buy so-and-so products to fix their flaws ... They're rejecting traditional forms of advertising that don't do anything but tear down your confidence."[43] Similarly, Dove launched a campaign called #InMyOwnSkin, where people can share their photos and personal stories as a way to inspire others who are living with skin conditions.

Having a strong support system is an important way to boost mental health and self-esteem. Daniel Boey was told when he was young that he could not be involved in the fashion industry because of the way he looked. However, he ignored these negative statements and went on to become highly successful. He has appeared as a judge on *Asia's Next Top Model* and earned the nickname "Godfather of Singapore Fashion" for his influence on the industry. In an interview, he talked about how encouragement from others helped him:

> *I've been told before that there is no place in fashion for someone like me, but that made me even more determined to prove everyone wrong. Thanks to an early mentor, who told me to create my own legacy, I was determined to do just that ...*
>
> *I realized that you can't buy respect and friendship. And if people choose not to associate with me because they are embarrassed to be seen with "the rashy one with sinus [problems]," then these shallow specimens are not people I really want in my life anyway! So I have chosen to surround myself with honest, down-to-earth folks.*[44]

Others agree that having a strong network of friends and family can make a difference. The magazine *NIH MedlinePlus* wrote about

Singaporean fashion director Daniel Boey (shown here) did not let eczema stop him from achieving success in the fashion world.

Kristin Donahue, who first experienced symptoms of psoriasis when she was five years old:

> *"Fortunately, I grew up in a small town in Oregon where everyone knew and accepted me,"* recalls Donahue, now 31, and a freelance writer. Surrounded by a loving family and understanding friends, she thrived emotionally and socially, swam freestyle on her high school swim team and never let psoriasis hold her back.

What Not to Say

Sometimes people try to be supportive of someone with a skin condition but accidentally say something unhelpful. Other times, lack of knowledge about a condition can lead someone to unknowingly say something hurtful. Below are some statements that are generally unhelpful for someone with a skin condition to hear:

- "It's not that bad. You're just being dramatic."

- "You're pretty even though you have [skin condition]."

- "Have you been to a dermatologist?"

- "You should try [diet/treatment/etc.]."

- "What's wrong with your skin?"

- "I know how you feel. My skin gets dry sometimes, too."

- "Stop scratching or you'll make it worse."

- "Why do you have to use special soap? You're so high maintenance."

- "At least you don't have a life-threatening disease."

While some people may be trying to be helpful by recommending products or treatments they have heard about, people with a chronic skin condition—especially one that is resistant to most treatments—often have worked with doctors to figure out what is good and bad for their skin. They generally do not need or want advice from people who are unfamiliar with the unique challenges that come with a skin disorder. Additionally, drawing attention to the way their skin looks is rude and hurtful; they are well aware of their condition, and asking about it or staring at it can make them feel embarrassed.

"But psoriasis can be very isolating," she says. "It's shaped me, made me a good judge of character." She credits her knack for finding people able to look beyond her physical condition with helping sustain her.[45]

Some people may not be able to accept someone because of the way their skin looks, but many other people can, and these are the ones a person should try to surround themselves with. Those who want to be a good friend to someone with a skin condition should learn what they can about the particular condition their friend has and encourage them to live their best life no matter what their skin looks like.

Along with a strong support system, people who have a skin condition can help improve their mental health by taking control of their disorder. Working closely with a dermatologist to minimize outbreaks can help make a patient feel less helpless about their condition. Boey offered this advice:

Life is what you make of it and you alone are responsible for how happy you want to feel. Find your own support system and your own coping mechanism. Couple that with a sensible lifestyle. Know what the triggers are and what forms of relief are out there. Knowledge is power, and the more knowledge you have of your condition, the better equipped you are to fight it. Having the right mindset is half the battle won already.[46]

Even the most loving friends and family members can have difficulty understanding what someone with a skin condition is going through, which is why support groups can be helpful. There, people can talk to others who have experienced the same things and exchange stories of what has worked for them personally. If there is no support group in a person's local area, they may be able to find one online.

Joining a support group can help people with a skin condition feel less isolated.

Unfortunately, there is no surefire cure for many chronic skin conditions. People can find the combination of treatments that help them manage their condition, but most learn to live with and accept their condition, knowing their mental health will suffer if they do not. In an article for BuzzFeed News, Lisa Ko wrote about her exhausting search for a cure for her severe eczema. She tried nearly every medical and alternative treatment in existence, including steroid creams, light therapy, acupuncture, wet wraps, an anti-inflammatory diet, and questionable alternative remedies: "I was instructed to sleep with my body covered in magnetic discs, tap my pulse points in a specific order, and stand facing a silver cone at 12-minute intervals."[47] The only things that worked were two drugs that she eventually had to stop taking because they caused more serious health problems. Eventually, Ko came to terms with the fact that management, not a cure, needed to be her goal. She wrote,

> When my skin gets better, *I thought*, then I'll do better. *Yet as long as the rash remained, I had an easy excuse for why I wasn't writing more or getting a better job. It was easier to believe I couldn't do these things because I had a rash than to risk trying and failing ... I believed nobody could love me when my face was red or my arms were flaky and peeling, but in all the years I'd had the rash, not a single person had stopped talking to me because of the way I looked ... I decided I would no longer fight it. There was nothing left to do, no miracle pill or cream or diet. There was only my poor immune system, my peeling face. And I was exhausted ...*
>
> *I wish I could say I found the magic cure and the rash never came back, but I can't. It remains there in varying degrees. It reasserts itself when I'm stressed, when I eat poorly, when I don't get enough sleep or try a new moisturizer or go into a hot tub or a swimming pool. But it's never returned for as long or as severely as it had before ... Perhaps the cure was to accept that there is no cure. You can only suppress a rash so much, for so long; you can't control its uncertainty. All you can do is try to accept its impermanence.*[48]

Through trial and error, Ko eventually found the balance of diet, moisturizer, and sleep that worked best to manage her flare-ups. Others may find that a particular medication works best for them. Also, by accepting that her eczema is a fact of her life and that people will love her regardless, Ko improved her mental health, learning to appreciate the good days when they come and reminding herself that the bad days will not last forever.

CHAPTER FIVE

LOOKING FORWARD

Although there is no cure for most chronic skin conditions, researchers continue to work toward finding new and better treatments that will provide more long-term relief. They are also looking further into the causes of certain skin conditions to create more targeted treatments.

Photodynamic Treatment

Photodynamic treatment (PDT) is a newer therapy that uses light to treat many different kinds of disorders. Some treatments also use a red or pink light afterward to reverse signs of aging and soothe the skin, reducing the redness that comes with acne. It works well for healing papules and pustules, but it cannot heal comedones or cysts. For this reason, dermatologists generally prescribe a topical ointment or cream in addition to PDT.

PDT sessions take time. Patients have to go to a dermatologist's office 2 to 3 times a week for about 12 weeks in order to see results. The length of each session can vary from 15 minutes to several hours, depending on the severity and location of the person's acne. During PDT, a photosensitizing drug is applied. According to *Medical News Today*, "Photosensitizers are topically applied solutions that cause certain types of abnormal cells to produce light-absorbing molecules called porphyrins.

This change allows the light treatment to target the abnormal cells that are contributing to acne."[49] The skin is dried, and after a short wait, the patient sits in front of a blue light. While being exposed to the light source used in PDT, the patient may feel warmth, tingling, or even a mild burning sensation.

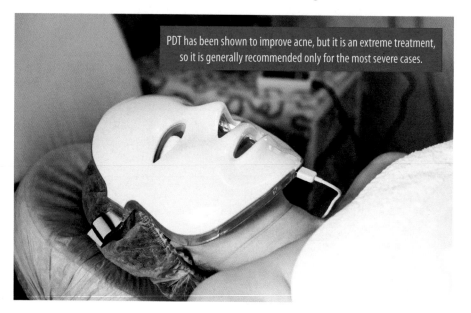

PDT has been shown to improve acne, but it is an extreme treatment, so it is generally recommended only for the most severe cases.

After PDT, the skin remains unusually sensitive to light for several days. Patients who receive PDT must be prepared to protect their skin rigorously from the sun for at least 48 hours after each treatment. Even using sunscreen is not enough protection. "I was given strict orders to avoid the sun for a few days," remembered Andrea Lavinthal, a patient who received the treatment. "When I did leave my apartment, I had to wear a hat, sunglasses, and a scarf ... Plus I was forbidden to wash or moisturize my face for four whole days ... my skin was red, raw, and drier than the Sahara [Desert]."[50]

PDT does produce good results for many acne sufferers. One study showed a 60 percent reduction in the number of pimples on patients' skin after

8 PDT sessions. The sebaceous glands shrink during PDT, and sebum production remains low for at least six months after the treatment. Lavinthal said that a month afterward, she felt her treatment was worth it—her acne was gone, her scars were much less noticeable, and she felt she could skip wearing makeup sometimes. However, it is expensive; each session costs between $100 and $400, and health insurance does not cover it. Since the results are not permanent, the patient will eventually have to go back for follow-up sessions. For this reason, many people who regularly get PDT are celebrities.

Other Types of Light

Other types of light therapy are available to treat different types of acne. Laser therapy is another new way to use light to treat acne. Laser light, though, is much higher in intensity than the blue light used for PDT. Laser light is pure, high-energy light. It is focused, meaning that the light is all one wavelength and all one frequency, and the crests and troughs of the waves travel together. Laser light is the only kind of light that has waves that are all the same and travel in sync with each other. This property of laser light is what makes it useful to doctors.

Lasers can be helpful for treating inflammatory acne, such as papules and pustules. Studies show that laser light can greatly reduce the number of acne lesions a patient has even after just one treatment. After four such treatments, the number of lesions drops even more dramatically. The improvements to the skin remain for at least six months. However, even though many people see improvements, laser therapy may not completely clear skin.

Another type of therapy is visible light therapy. It uses blue light, red light, or a combination of both to treat pimples. The blue light kills the bacteria on the skin, and the red light soothes skin and reduces redness. It is expensive, but there are at-home options available. They are less powerful than the lights a dermatologist uses, but they can be used more consistently because the person does not have to make time to go to the doctor's office. This consistency may help people see results more quickly.

As of 2018, the cheapest at-home mask is the Neutrogena Light Therapy Acne Mask. *Allure* and *People* magazines tested it; both testers determined that, combined with their regular skin care routine, their skin seemed to be getting clearer, but they could not say for certain that it was because of the mask. *People*'s tester, Maria Yagoda, noted, "With skin care, changes can be hard to understand because there are so many factors to consider. (How clean are your pillow cases? Are you stressed? What are you eating? Are you touching your face obsessively?)"[51]

A third option, called photopneumatic therapy, is a type of light therapy that "combines an intense pulsed light (IPL) with a gentle vacuum. It works by removing excess oil and dead skin cells from clogged pores."[52] It can treat blackheads, whiteheads, and some pimples, but it is ineffective against nodules and cysts.

Lasers have also become a way to treat acne scars, but they have some drawbacks. The area that has been treated with the laser must be covered with a bandage until it is entirely healed, and it is not a good option for people who are still getting breakouts. A more common and effective treatment for scars is dermabrasion, which uses a rough material such as a wire brush to smooth away the top layers of skin mechanically. It is like sanding the skin. Dermabrasion damages the skin—especially for people with darker skin—and it can be painful. Afterward, the skin may look and feel as though it has been badly sunburned. After dermabrasion, it takes about 10 days for the skin to heal. At first, the new skin is pink, but after two or three months, it looks like normal skin again. Laser treatment works on the same principle but has a shorter healing time.

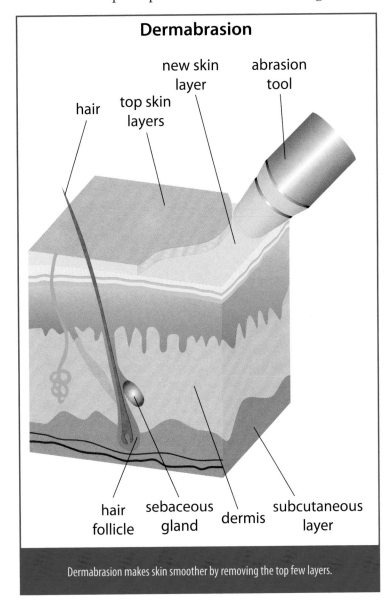

Dermabrasion

new skin layer

abrasion tool

hair

top skin layers

hair follicle

sebaceous gland

dermis

subcutaneous layer

Dermabrasion makes skin smoother by removing the top few layers.

Biologics

Since eczema and psoriasis have genetic causes, they can be treated with genetic therapies. The NEA explained what biologics are and how they work:

> Biologic drugs, or "biologics," are among the most targeted therapies available today because they essentially use human DNA to treat certain diseases at the immune system level. Taken subcutaneously (through the skin) or intravenously (in the vein), biologics are genetically engineered medications that contain proteins derived from living tissues or cells cultured in a laboratory.
>
> The human body contains a certain type of protein called an interleukin, or IL, that helps our immune system fight off harmful viruses and bacteria. But for people with inflammatory diseases like atopic dermatitis, the immune system overreacts and triggers certain ILs to respond by producing inflammation … Biologics block ILs from binding to their cell receptors, which stops the immune system from overreacting.[1]

As of 2018, only two biologic medications are approved by the FDA. Like most systemic treatments, they are meant for adults who have moderate or severe eczema or psoriasis who have tried or are unable to use other treatments. The first medication to be approved is called dupilumab and is marketed under the brand name Dupixent.

The old scars may not be gone, but their appearance and texture should improve. Dermabrasion cannot be done on people who have taken isotretinoin in the past year.

New Eczema Treatments

Recent research into people's microbiomes has given researchers new ideas about how to treat eczema. "Microbiome" is the word for all the natural, helpful bacteria that live in people's bodies. One 2018 study suggests that taking bacteria from the skin of people without eczema and putting them on the skin of someone who has the disease may change the skin microbiome enough to relieve their symptoms. In the study, the participants sprayed a

This medication treats eczema. According to the NEA, "In clinical trials, more than half of patients using Dupixent for 16 weeks reported their symptoms of atopic dermatitis were reduced by 75 percent."[2] Patients must go to their doctor every other week to receive a subcutaneous injection of Dupixent. It has limited side effects, including pink eye, cold sores on the mouth, and irritation near the injection site. The second medication is called certolizumab pegol (brand name Cimzia), and it treats psoriasis and psoriatic arthritis. Like Dupixent, it is given through subcutaneous injection and has had good results in clinical trials.

Further research is being done in this area, and in May 2018, a study by the Washington University School of Medicine found that a modified version of a naturally produced compound called itaconate showed results in mice. Previous studies "had shown that inflammatory cells that detect the presence of bacteria produce itaconate. But surprisingly, rather than amplifying inflammation, itaconate dampens it."[3] The researchers changed itaconate slightly to create dimethyl itaconate, then injected the new compound into mice with psoriasis-like symptoms. The compound cleared up the mice's symptoms after a week. The researchers found that dimethyl itaconate reduces levels of a protein that plays a key role in autoimmune diseases. The researchers hope that by targeting this protein, they can treat not only psoriasis and psoriatic arthritis but also other autoimmune diseases such as multiple sclerosis and lupus.

1. "Biologics," National Eczema Association, accessed on April 25, 2018. nationaleczema.org/eczema/treatment/dupixent.

2. "Biologics," National Eczema Association.

3. News Staff, "Compound Derived from Immune Cells Treats Psoriasis in Mice," *SciNews*, May 8, 2018. www.sci-news.com/medicine/dimethyl-itaconate-psoriasis-05984.html.

solution of sugar water that contained bacteria taken from people without eczema onto their skin several times a week. They also continued using their normal eczema treatments. After a few weeks, most of the participants reported a 50 percent reduction in symptoms, and some were able to cut back on the amount of steroid cream they had been using. This study was small, but the researchers hope a larger study will show similar results.

Other studies, one of which was sponsored by the National Eczema Association, have found that relief may come from a surprising source: marijuana. Smoking it will not have any effect, but when it is turned into an ointment, it may reduce the itching and redness associated with eczema without producing the high that comes with smoking the plant. More studies must be done, however, to determine what long-term effects the ointment might have. Research has been difficult so far because until recently, marijuana was illegal throughout the United States, and it is still illegal in some states. For this reason, marijuana ointments are not yet prescribed by many doctors. Some websites advertise them, but the entertainment website LADbible offered an important warning: "We wouldn't advise trying to order anything off the internet—there's no way to know what else might be in the cream you're ordering."[53]

While there may never be a magical cure for most skin conditions, these new treatments may offer relief to people whose disease resists the ones that are currently available. Additionally, new breakthroughs may treat conditions such as eczema and psoriasis in a way that causes fewer negative side effects than steroid creams and other current options. More research is needed, but the future looks promising.

Introduction:
Understanding Skin Conditions

1. "Cellulitis," Healthline, accessed on April 17, 2018. www.healthline.com/health/cellulitis.

2. Quoted in Mary Brophy Marcus, "Acne Leaves Emotional Marks," *USA Today*, February 12, 2007, p. 07d.

3. Ted Grossbart, "The Emotional Impact of Skin Problems," *Psychology Today*, January 9, 2010. www.psychologytoday.com/us/blog/skin-deep/201001/the-emotional-impact-skin-problems.

4. Quoted in Samantha Critchell, "New Treatments Popping Up for Adults with Acne," *Toronto Star*, March 7, 2008, p. L03.

Chapter One:
Symptoms of Common Conditions

5. Quoted in Lydia Preston and Tina Alster, *Breaking Out*. New York, NY: Simon & Schuster, 2004, p. 31.

6. Staff Writer, "Severe Acne: Nodular Acne and Acne Cysts," Acne.com, accessed on April 18, 2018. www.acne.com/types-of-acne/nodules-and-cysts.

7. Gary W. Cole, "Eczema," MedicineNet, March 15, 2018. www.medicinenet.com/eczema_facts/index.htm.

8. "What Is Psoriasis?," Psoriasis.com, accessed on April 18, 2018. www.psoriasis.com/what-is-psoriasis.

9. "About Psoriasis," National Psoriasis Foundation, accessed on April 18, 2018. www.psoriasis.org/about-psoriasis.

Chapter Two:
Causes of Common Conditions

10. Quoted in "Dermatologists Caution that Atopic Dermatitis Is a Strong Precursor to Food Allergies," American Academy of Dermatology, February 4, 2011. www.aad.org/media/news-releases/dermatologists-caution-that-atopic-dermatitis-is-a-strong-precursor-to-food-allergies.

11. Lynda Schneider, "Eczema, Atopic Dermatitis and Allergies: What Is the Connection?," National Eczema Association, accessed on April 19, 2018. nationaleczema.org/atopic-dermatitis-and-allergies-connection.

12. David Zelman, "Psoriatic Arthritis: The Basics," WebMD, August 29, 2016. www.webmd.com/arthritis/psoriatic-arthritis/psoriatic-arthritis-the-basics#3.

13. Quoted in Maria Masters, "9 Things You Should Never Do If You Have Eczema," *Health*, April 27, 2017. www.health.com/eczema/eczema-triggers.

14. Ana Sandoiu, "Scientists Find Genetic Under-pinnings for Eczema," *Medical News Today*, June 21, 2017. www.medicalnewstoday.com/articles/318024.php.

15. "Genes and Psoriasis," National Psoria-sis Foundation, accessed on April 20, 2018. www.psoriasis.org/research/genes-and-psoriatic-disease.

Chapter Three:
Treatment for Common Conditions

16. Richard Fried, *Healing Adult Acne*. Oakland, CA: New Harbinger, 2005, p. 29.

17. Quoted in Simone Kitchens, "Toothpaste to Dry Out Pimples? Top Derms Clear Up this Home Remedy," *Huffington Post*, October 25, 2012. www.huffingtonpost.com/2012/10/23/toothpaste-pimples-acne-dry-out_n_1994320.html.

18. Quoted in Preston and Alster, *Breaking Out*, p. 64.

19. Quoted in Preston and Alster, *Breaking Out*, p. 43.

20. Quoted in Paul Swiech, "Acne Solutions," Pantagraph, September 15, 2006. search.ebscohost.com/login.aspx?direct=direct=true&db=nfh&AN=262W61157203880&site=ehost-live.

21. Fried, *Healing Adult Acne*, p. 23.

22. Fried, *Healing Adult Acne*, p. 55.

23. Chrishell Stause, "A Proactiv Solution Success Story," Proactiv. www.proactiv.com/celebrity/chrishell-stause.php.

24. "Eczema Treatment," National Eczema Association, accessed on April 20, 2018. nationaleczema.org/eczema/treatment.

25. "Eczema and Bathing," National Eczema Association, accessed on April 25, 2018. nationaleczema.org/eczema/treatment/bathing.

26. "Prescription Topical Treatment," National Eczema Association, accessed on April 25, 2018. nationaleczema.org/eczema/treatment/topicals.

27. "Prescription Topical Treatment," National Eczema Association.

28. "Prescription Topical Treatment," National Eczema Association.

29. "Phototherapy," National Eczema Association, accessed on April 25, 2018. nationaleczema.org/eczema/treatment/phototherapy.

30. Andrew Wright, "Systemic Treatments for Severe Eczema in Adults and Children," *Exchange*, p. 20.

31. "Systemic Medications: Methotrexate," National Psoriasis Foundation, accessed on April 25, 2018. www.psoriasis.org/about-psoriasis/treatments/systemics/methotrexate.

32. Billie Sahley, "Acne and Other Skin Problems," MMRC Health Educator Reports, 2008, pp. 1–2.

33. Quoted in Karrie Osborn, "Guided Imagery and Massage," *Massage & Bodywork*, May/June 2008. www.massagetherapy.com/articles/index.php/article_id/1568/Guided-Imagery-and-Massage.

34. Quoted in Osborn, "Guided Imagery and Massage."

35. Quoted in Amy Stork, "Can Diet Heal Psoriasis?," National Psoriasis Foundation, September 10, 2015. www.psoriasis.org/advance/can-diet-heal-psoriasis.

Chapter Four:
Living with a Skin Condition

36. Jennie Lyon, "The Stigma of Eczema in the News," AD RescueWear, June 17, 2016. www.adrescuewear.com/blog/the-stigma-of-eczema-in-the-news.

37. Lyon, "The Stigma of Eczema in the News."

38. Quoted in Kathryn Jones, "Eczema En Vogue: Fighting the Stigma in Fashion," National Eczema Association, December 18, 2017. nationaleczema.org/eczema-en-vogue.

39. Stephanie S. Gardner, "The Emotional Toll of Psoriasis," WebMD, January 15, 2018. www.webmd.com/skin-problems-and-treatments/psoriasis/coping-with-psoriasis#1.

40. Quoted in Katie Rodan, Kathy Fields, and Vanessa Williams, *Unblemished*. New York, NY: Simon & Schuster, 2004, p. 66.

41. Serena Williams, "A Proactiv Solution Success Story," Proactiv. www.proactiv.com/celebrity/serena-williams.php.

42. Jessica Simpson, "A Proactiv Solution Success Story," Proactiv. www.proactiv.com/celebrity/jessica-simpson.php.

43. Quoted in Andrea Cheng, "Is Acne Cool Now?," *New York Times*, May 28, 2018. www.nytimes.com/2018/05/28/style/is-acne-cool-now.html.

44. Quoted in Jones, "Eczema En Vogue."

45. "I Live with Psoriasis," *NIH MedlinePlus*, Fall 2013. medlineplus.gov/magazine/issues/fall13/articles/fall13pg22-23.html.

46. Quoted in Jones, "Eczema En Vogue."

47. Lisa Ko, "How I Learned to Live with a Chronic Skin Condition," BuzzFeed News, May 2, 2017. www.buzzfeed.com/lisako/my-atopia?utm_term=.nijz1QAKd#.dbZm5Qa6g.

48. Ko, "How I Learned to Live with a Chronic Skin Condition."

Chapter Five: Looking Forward

49. Jayne Leonard, "Photodynamic Therapy for Acne: Costs and Recovery," *Medical News Today*, last updated September 5, 2017. www.medicalnewstoday.com/articles/319256.php.

50. Andrea Lavinthal, "The Crazy Thing I Did for Clear Skin," *Cosmopolitan*, March 18, 2009. www.cosmopolitan.com/hairstyles-beauty/beauty-blog/clear-skin-treatment?-click=main_sr.

51. Maria Yagoda, "We Tried It: That Weird-Looking, Acne-Blasting Light Mask that Celebs Are Obsessed With," *People*, January 18, 2017. people.com/beauty/neutrogena-acne-mask-review.

52. "Lasers and Lights: How Well Do They Treat Acne?," American Academy of Dermatology, accessed on June 4, 2018. www.aad.org/public/diseases/acne-and-rosacea/lasers-and-lights-how-well-do-they-treat-acne.

53. Daisy Jackson, "Marijuana Could Be the Solution to Your Eczema Problems," LADbible, June 1, 2018. www.ladbible.com/community/news-marijuana-could-be-the-solution-to-your-eczema-problems-20180601.

alternative medicine: A non-drug approach to healing that emphasizes lifestyle changes, such as a healthy diet, exercise, and rest, and uses natural remedies when medical intervention is needed.

androgens: Hormones, such as testosterone, that are found at higher levels in men than in women.

antibiotics: Drugs that kill bacteria.

benzoyl peroxide: An antibacterial drug that is applied to the surface of the skin.

comedo: A plug made of dead epidermal skin cells.

comedo extraction: The process of removing or draining the contents of a blackhead, whitehead, or cyst.

comedone: A blemish formed when a hair follicle is blocked by a comedo.

dermabrasion: The process of mechanically rubbing off or sanding away the top layers of skin.

dermatologist: A doctor specializing in the diagnosis and treatment of skin disorders.

dermis: The middle layer of the skin.

epidermis: The outer layer of the skin.

hormones: Chemicals produced by the body's glands and released as a signal to tell cells and tissues in another part of the body to do something.

inflammation: Redness and swelling.

photodynamic treatment (PDT): Therapy that uses light and a photosensitizing agent to treat acne.

puberty: A developmental stage in which the hypothalamus and pituitary glands release hormones governing sexual development.

retinoids: Drugs that come from vitamin A.

salicylic acid: An exfoliant and anti-inflammatory drug that can be applied to the surface of the skin.

sebaceous glands: Glands that produce sebum, or oil.

subcutaneous tissue: Also known as the hypodermis, the deepest layer of skin, containing the fat that cushions the body against bumps and falls.

American Academy of Dermatology
P.O. Box 1968
Des Plaines, IL 60017
(888) 462-3376
www.aad.org
The American Academy of Dermatology represents
nearly all dermatologists in the United States. It
publishes several magazines and journals, offers
referrals to dermatologists, produces press releases and
fact sheets, advocates on behalf of dermatologists when
federal and state legislation related to skin care is being
considered, and offers information to the general public
on its website.

American Skin Association
335 Madison Avenue, 22nd Floor
New York, NY 10017
(212) 889-4858
info@americanskin.org
www.americanskin.org
The goals of this nonprofit organization are to raise
public awareness of skin cancer and other diseases,
promote skin health, and advance medical research.

National Eczema Association
4460 Redwood Highway, Suite 16-D
San Rafael, CA 94903
(415) 499-3474
nationaleczema.org
This organization researches causes of and treatment for
eczema. It also advocates for eczema patients.

National Institute of Arthritis and Musculoskeletal and Skin Diseases
NIAMS Information Clearinghouse
National Institutes of Health
Bethesda, MD 20892
(301) 495-4484
niamsinfo@mail.nih.gov
www.niams.nih.gov
The National Institute of Arthritis and Musculoskeletal and Skin Diseases is a department of the National Institutes of Health, which is part of the U.S. Department of Health and Human Services. Health specialists are available to answer questions Monday through Friday from 8:00 a.m. to 5:00 p.m., although they are not able to make diagnoses or give medical advice. The website includes information about common and uncommon skin disorders.

National Psoriasis Foundation
6600 SW 92nd Avenue, Suite 300
Portland, OR 97223
(800) 723-9166
getinfo@psoriasis.org
www.psoriasis.org
This nonprofit organization is committed to finding cures for psoriasis and improving the lives of patients.

Books

De Meza, Lesley, and Stephen De Silva. *The A–Z of Growing Up, Puberty and Sex*. London, UK: Franklin Watts, 2014.
Among other things, the authors discuss common skin conditions that tend to appear when someone reaches puberty.

Ehrlich, Fred, and Amanda Haley. *You Can't Take Your Body to a Car Mechanic!* Maplewood, NJ: Blue Apple Books, 2014.
This book includes two chapters on skin conditions, including acne, warts, and blisters.

Sherman, Rebecca. *Allergies and Other Immune System Disorders*. Broomall, PA: Mason Crest, 2018.
The author looks at different types of disorders that affect the immune system, including eczema.

Webster, Guy, and Anthony Rawlings. *Acne and Its Therapy*. Boca Raton, FL: CRC, 2007.
This is a collection of scientific and detailed articles on different aspects of acne, such as the formation of comedones, retinoid treatment, light therapy, and the use of benzoyl peroxide and salicylic acid.

Woolf, Alex. *The Science of Acne and Warts: The Itchy Truth About Skin*. New York, NY: Franklin Watts, 2018.
The author explores the causes of common skin problems and discusses why skin is such an important part of the way a person views their appearance.

Websites

Allure: Skin

www.allure.com/skin-care
Allure magazine's skin care blog includes sections that give advice about acne, makeup, dermatologists, and more. It also promotes body positivity with articles such as "Living in My Skin: 8 People Reveal Why They Love Their Freckles, Moles, and More."

BrainPOP: Immune System

www.brainpop.com/health/bodysystems/immunesystem
Learn more about the immune system through games, activities, and videos.

Healthline: "All About Common Skin Disorders"

www.healthline.com/health/skin-disorders#pictures
This article lists several common disorders along with photos to help someone identify something they might be experiencing. Links to more in-depth articles about each disorder are included.

TeensHealth: Skin Stuff

kidshealth.org/en/teens/your-body/?WT.ac=t-nav-your-body
This section of the TeensHealth website includes articles about many different skin topics, including acne, dandruff, eczema, vitiligo, and basic skin care.

INDEX

PICTURE CREDITS

ABOUT THE AUTHOR

Donna Reynolds is a freelance writer and editor who has worked on more than 50 books for young adults. She has a degree in English from the University of Wisconsin–Madison and spends as much time as possible traveling around the world. She tries to volunteer at a local nonprofit organization at least one day a week, no matter where she happens to be. Researching this book helped her understand more about her own struggle with psoriasis.